# MAGIC STEPS TO WRITING SUCCESS

## by

## Charles W. Sasser

*MAGIC STEPS TO WRITING SUCCESS by* Charles W. Sasser

An original publication of AWOC.COM, P O Box 2819, Denton, TX 76202

ISBN: 0-9707507-5-7

Visit the web site of Charles W. Sasser at *CharlesSasser.com*

**Also by Charles W. Sasser**

**Nonfiction**

*The Walking Dead (with Craig Roberts)*
*Homicide!*
*Shoot To Kill*
*One Shot-One Kill (with Craig Roberts)*
*Always A Warrior*
*Last American Heroes (with Michael Sasser)*
*In Cold Blood: Oklahoma's Most Notorious Murders*
*Smoke Jumpers*
*First SEAL (with Roy Boehm)*
*Doc: Platoon Medic (with Daniel E. Evans)*
*Fire Cops (with Michael Sasser)*
*At Large*
*Arctic Homestead (with Norma Cobb)*
*Taking Fire (with Ron Alexander)*
*Raider*
*Encyclopedia Of Navy SEALs*
*Hill 488 (with Ray Hildreth)*
*Pathways: Magic Steps To Writing Success*

**Novels**

*No Gentle Streets*
*The 100th Kill*
*Operation No Man's Land (writing as Mike Martell)*
*Liberty City*
*The Return*
*Detachment Delta: Operation Punitive Strike*
*Detachment Delta: Operation Iron Weed*
*Detachment Delta: Operation Deep Steel*

**Booklets**

*Last Stage To Bondage*
*How to Earn a Living In Adventure*
*The Lonely Circle of Light*

4

**Contributing Author**

*The Soldier of Fortune*
*Sky Soldiers*
*Commando Operations*
*Mass Murderers*
*Family Slaughters*
*Killer Teens*
*Greed Killers*
*Stranglers*
*Sex Sadists*
*Spouse Killers*
*Predators*
*Unsolved Mysteries*
*Cult Killers*
*Serial Murderers*

# Table of Contents

This book is dedicated to my mom, Mary, who once built me a desk; to Donna Sue, who understands how hard it is to be a writer; and to Ethan Ellenberg, who helped make the dream.

*"I've told you how very hard writing is because it is. But I haven't told you this to discourage you. I've told you to encourage you. Because if you're frustrated with your writing, if you're growing pessimistic, if you are sometimes visited with despair as I was—that sickening feeling that you could write forever and never get published—then perhaps it is because you thought learning to write well was going to be easy."*

*— Gary Provost*

# INTRODUCTION

My dad, a product of the Great Depression, could neither read nor write. He quit school in the second grade and went through much of his life in the dark. My mom completed the eighth grade before she quit. We were so poor during much of my youth that even poverty was a step up. Virtually the only books we had in our house were *Sears & Roebuck* catalogues, and only those because of their utilitarian value in the outhouse.

When I was six or seven years old, my great aunt Ellen Rossen gave me a box of books, among which were classics by Hemingway, Steinbeck, Defoe and others. I began to read. I read *everything*. It was like books opened up a fresh new world outside cotton fields and strawberry patches and three-room shacks in the woods.

I began writing. I wrote a novel when I was eight years old. I earned my first money from writing at age 15--$25 from a contest sponsored by a local newspaper.

"You mean you can get *paid* for writing?"

I was hooked. Like the authors of my wonderful books, I was going to live my life and earn my livelihood as a writer. Never would I have to live life in the dark as my dad had.

In 1979, the year I turned 37, I was a big-city cop, a homicide detective. I resigned to become a full-time freelance writer/journalist/photographer. My then-wife's relatives were appalled.

"Divorce that fool!" they advised. "Tell him to go back and get a *real* job."

I have since published about 40 books, at least 2,500 magazine articles and short stories, several educational films, hundreds of newspaper articles, and one of my books became the basis for a movie starring Tom Berringer. My books have been translated into a number of different languages, including Chinese and Russian, and my biography is included in *Who's Who In America* and *Who's Who In The World*. I've adventure-traveled the globe writing pieces for publications such as *Soldier Of Fortune* and *Time/Life*. In 1985, I was a finalist to fly into space with NASA's Journalist-in-Space project. I now live on an Oklahoma horse ranch where I rear and train registered quarter horses. Not bad for a "good ole boy" who grew up in cotton fields.

The tool shed in which I lived when I first became a full-time writer. With second wife Kathy and adopted son Joshua.

If a poor hill kid from an illiterate background can earn a good living at writing, so can you.

There is no mystery as such to becoming successful as a writer, no big secrets. There is, however, a sort of magic, a pathway of magic steps. Unless you learn the basis of this magic and how to develop and use it, you should be properly content in your career to scribble down about anything when the mood strikes and shove it into a bottom drawer for posterity or the trash man, whichever comes first. But if you long to *publish* what you write, to *become* a writer, then perhaps I can help you find that magic pathway.

Visit any major book store and browse the Reference section, where you will find scores of books on *how* to write. How to write the mystery, the suspense, the romance, science fiction, westerns... Books on how to plot and how to build characters. Volumes on developing the scribbler's craft—on how to get ideas, develop style, use foreshadowing and plants, employ scenes and sequels, manage narrative, utilize dialogue...

While all of this is helpful, of course, what is generally neglected is how to *become* a writer, how to *be* a writer. There is more to becoming a writer than knowing how to outline a plot or write good dialogue. Craft is the nuts and bolts of the engine that makes the magic work. However, before the automobile could run on a freeway at 70 mph or a jetliner hop from New York to London came the *concept* of the internal combustion engine, the *concept* of horseless travel and of flight. Without those concepts, there would never have been an automobile or an airplane or any of the technological comforts we take for granted.

You cannot *be* a writer unless you first develop the concept of what is necessary to *become* a writer. In this book, I hope to help you find the pathway by exploring the five magic steps toward becoming a successful writer—Discipline; Inspiration; Goals; Ideas; and Craft. In the end, you will find that the magic you develop is inside yourself. Ultimately, *you* determine your own success or failure.

# SECTION I:
# Discipline

*"First, there must be talent, much talent. Talent such as Kipling had. Then there must be discipline, the discipline of Flaubert."*

— *Ernest Hemingway*

Writing in my lonely circle of light, always up before dawn to work. At my apartment in Tulsa between marriages.

# CHAPTER ONE

"Don't you have to have talent? How do you know if you have talent?"

These questions in one form or another are almost always asked whenever I speak at writers conferences or to writers groups. Taking a cue from Socrates, I answer by telling about a friend of mine who wanted to be a writer. I met Ken when I served a hitch in the U.S. Navy as a journalist, feature writer for a military newspaper called *Prop Wash*. Ken, a reporter on the same paper, was brilliant. He had a truck load of talent, more talent than I could even dream of.

Although Ken possessed ambition, he lacked an essential ingredient that would have enabled him to realize his goals. Ken had no discipline. He slothed around until deadline approached, then put in a coffee-pot all-nighter to get his copy in on time. He freelanced a short story now and then, whenever he felt *inspired*, but no editor could count on him. Ken couldn't even count on Ken. His philosophy seemed to go something like: "What's the advantage of being a writer if I have to work so hard at it?"

On the other hand, I arrived at the *Prop Wash* office two hours early every morning to work on my short stories and novels. In addition to my duties for the newspaper, I was also burning oil learning the writer's craft. I was receiving bucketsful of rejection, which I promptly tossed into the circular file. I have never understood why writers collect rejection slips, which serve only to remind them of their failures.

"Sasser, why don't you give up?" Ken chided. "Lets face it— you don't have the talent."

Give up? Maybe I wasn't smart enough to give up. I kept plugging away. Every day. Laboring to realize a dream I had nurtured since I was a kid. I was going to be a writer, come hell or high water, as my old grandpa used to say.

From the time I was six years old I was out in the fields picking cotton, helping with the planting, driving an old brown mule named Jude up and down the furrows with my grandpa. Milking cows, working the garden, building fence. Everyone in the family worked. We were semi-migrant workers in that we followed the crops around Oklahoma and Arkansas. Cotton. Spinach. Strawberries. We moved a lot with the harvests; we had no real roots. At various times, we occupied a dirt-floored chicken house, an old barn in Burns Flat, Oklahoma, and once lived in a house the rent for which was ten dollars a *year*.

I learned the value of discipline before I learned to either read or write. The year my Aunt Ellen gave me that box of books, thereby opening up my world beyond cotton fields and the rear end of a mule, we lived in a three-room shack in the woods of what we called the "ticky place." Ticks were thicker than lice on a coyote. The shack was unpainted and hadn't been lived in for over twenty years. It wasn't a house; it was the hull of a house, its ghost. We took old tarpaper and anything else we could find and tacked it on the boards inside as insulation. In the winter, snow and ice blew underneath the door and halfway across the living room. The cane heater stove ate up firewood and roared to stave off the chill.

There was a living room about ten feet by twenty, a smaller bedroom in the middle, and a kitchen to balance out the other end. There was no plumbing; water came from a dug well a quarter-mile from the house. Two beds fit in the bedroom, one on either side of a narrow walkway that connected the living room and kitchen. We hung our clothing on strands of baling wire stretched above the beds. Mom and Dad slept in one bed. Joe and Kenneth, my two younger brothers, and I slept in the other bed. I got my own personal, private bed when I enlisted in the navy.

I was about seven or eight when Mom built me a desk out of old boards and vegetable crates and placed it in a corner of the kitchen. That was the start of my discipline as a writer. Every morning I was up by four a.m. I built a fire in the heater to warm up the house, then hurried to my desk. Where, wrapped in a blanket to keep warm, in the light of a kerosene lamp, I went all over the world in my imagination. Writing about adventures I would have one day, exploring what small talent a ragged little hill kid might possess.

In front of the "ticky place" shack where Mom built my first desk and I began writing.

"I'm not gonna pick cotton," I assured my mother. 'I'm gonna be a famous writer and travel all over the world. I'm not gonna live one life. I'm gonna live many lives and write about them."

Mom remained tolerant, Dad mocking. Unable to read, he therefore couldn't comprehend *writing*.

"What you had better do, boy," he scoffed, "is get you a good high school education and get you a good job. Like out at the cresote plant or something."

I ignored him and kept writing. Every day. I wrote a complete novel, *Devil Mountain.*

CHAPTER ONE –
Deep, restful silence hung over the small Indian village, Araugas, in Venezuela, South America, like a veil of clouds over an Andes Mountain peak. The silence was so pronounced that it could even be touched with the hand if one so desired. But who was there to desire? It was midday, words which represented heat and insects and laziness. Only one person was evident in the narrow pathway among the native huts—an old, withered Indian man brown and cracked like old shoe leather...

Give me a break. I was only eight years old.

I wrote erotic stories in high school and sold them to other hormone-raging teen boys. I started my own book report business. If you didn't read, I wrote a book report for you for fifty cents or a dollar. Many of the books on which I reported didn't even exist. I created them, titles, authors, characters and plots. In a sense, I suppose, I was already a professional. Wasn't I writing for money?

When I was fifteen years old, the Sequoyah County *Times* sponsored a writing contest that changed my life. Entrants were required to write an essay on some aspect of living in Oklahoma. I wrote on a topic I knew well—cotton fields—and won what at that time was an amazing prize of $25, considering I was making about three dollars a day picking cotton from sunup to sundown.

"You mean you can *really* get paid for writing?"

Somehow, I must have known you could, but it had never occurred to me that it would be so *easy.* And such big money. Dad looked at the check, held it right side up and upside down and had Mom read it to him. Mom was hand ironing clothes in a laundry six days a week and earning about twelve dollars. Dad made less than thirty dollars a week laboring at the cresote plant.

Dad shook his head disbelievingly and walked off. I returned to my desk—and it was never that easy again to earn big money. But it demonstrated to me that it *could* be done. All I had to do was stay at my desk, get up and write every morning. No matter what.

"Any man who keeps working is not a failure," Ray Bradbury said. "He may not be a great writer, but if he applies the old-fashioned virtues of hard, constant labor, he'll eventually make some kind of career for himself as a writer."

Great talent, I was discovering, may not be necessary to be a successful writer. Discipline is. Ken might have had the most talent, but I had the most discipline and perseverance. That made the difference. Today, I am a multi-published author. Ken has yet to publish anything significant. He has a *real* job in California, putting in his eight hours a day.

As a teenager roaming the Ozark Mountains

# CHAPTER TWO

Talent certainly helps, but the basis of a writer's success is not great talent. More vital than that, more essential, is your willingness to write, your desire to write, in fact your inability not to write. Writing successfully requires hard work, stern discipline, dedication to craft, faith in yourself—all of which must be developed, cultivated and nurtured in order to ultimately grow anything for the harvesting.

While serving with the U.S. Navy, I established the foundation for writing success both in the discipline required to meet newspaper deadlines and in the hands-on, personal-involvement type of writing I soon came to call "participatory journalism." In addition to feature writing for *Prop Wash*, I volunteered to write and edit the monthly aviation safety bulletin for Naval Air Station, Whidbey Island, Washington. The bulletin opened up even more opportunities by providing me access to fly naval aircraft anywhere, anytime I wanted.

I became a traveling journalist. I participated. Then I wrote features about my participation. Living many lives, just as I had told Mom when I was a kid. I landed with A-3D Skywarriors on aircraft carriers, spent time on destroyers and submarines, flew patrols looking for enemy (Soviet) submarines, hopped flights to different parts of the world. I attended the U.S. Marine Corps Survival and POW School, became photographer for a Navy SAR (search and rescue) team, trained as a boxer, organized a navy cowboy rodeo team... If anything was happening, I was there with my note pad and trusty Crowngraphic press camera. It was good training.

I was discharged in 1964 after serving four years. It would have been easy to re-up. But I hadn't sat all those years at my vegetable crate desk Mom built for me just to let my dreams go up in a puff. Too much security, I realized, eventually eroded discipline and weakened one's desires and ambitions, replaced them with something new and easier.

Using my mustering out pay and some savings, I bought a new 80cc Yamaha motorbike and loaded everything I owned on the back of it—a change of jeans, underwear, a couple of shirts, toiletries, a tent and sleeping bag, a portable Underwood-Olivetti typewriter, a Canon 35mm camera, and a few books—and set out from Whidbey Island to see the world, have some adventures, and write about them.

"The Navy's loss in this case is not only America's gain, but the entire world's," *Prop Wash* gushed on the day I departed. "Sound like a Hollywood buildup so far? Not if you know Sasser, have seen his unlimited reservoir of energy, and his comprehensive self-education and planning toward some lofty goals... Don't put money against him. It's going to take an immovable object to stop this irresistible force, and then don't count on it."

I was nothing if not stubborn.

I dubbed the motorbike *Odyssey*. Loaded, it had a top speed of about 45mph, much less than that against a headwind or going uphill. For the next year, I traveled in Canada, the U.S., and Mexico, living in the tent. Every morning, no matter where I happened to be, I rolled out of my sleeping bag, built a campfire, and knocked out two hours of writing. It was a ritual from which I rarely deviated.

One morning when I was camped in the mesquite flatlands of Idaho, a cowboy rode up, dismounted, and squatted next to the fire. We had coffee together and he looked over my motorbike.

"Where you headed, son?" he asked.

"I don't know. I'm going to be a writer."

"A rider? You looking for a cowboying job?"

"No, sir. A *writer*. Like books and magazines."

"Oh," he said. "How do you do that?"

"I work at it every day," I said. "I just keep plugging away."

He looked at me. He looked at my tent. "Seems like a tough row to hoe," he said.

I was camped in an abandoned churchyard in Piauve, Mississippi, the night the FBI arrested Sheriff Rainey and the others involved in the slayings of three civil rights activists. A crowd of men and boys gathered in front of a little country store a hundred yards or so up the road. The mob started my way. I slipped a Bowie knife into the back waistband of my jeans, fearing I was going to have to fight my way out of this.

Arriving in Miami, Florida, after traveling for a year on this motorbike, living in a tent.

A cracker with two missing teeth and a family tree that looked to have only one branch spat a stream of tobacco juice at the tire of my motorbike. A big sow pig rooted around for acorns nearby.

"Boy," said the cracker, "that ole pig could eat you up tonight and nobody'd ever know what happened to you."

I did some quick grinning and fast talking on those good ole boys. I didn't figure it an appropriate time to mention that I had joined the NAACP, a white guy's auxiliary, because I thought it wrong to discriminate against people because of the color of their skins. Soon, it came out that I was a writer and that, no, I wasn't writing about civil rights in the South.

"Well, boy, ya hongra?"

"Huh?"

"He's asking do you want something to eat, do you?"

I was always hungry.

"Come on to the house, boy, and I'll see the ole lady fixes you something."

I would like to say I earned enough money writing about my adventures to provide for my needs while I kept moving. Truth is, I made ten bucks here, twenty there, mostly by writing articles for smaller newspapers and "little" magazines that often paid only in contributor copies. Even considering my meager needs and wants, I certainly never earned enough to keep hamburgers coming in. I had to get temporary jobs here and there.

I slung hash in Salt Lake City, ran a printing press in Tulsa, sold my oil paintings in New Orleans (I thought I was also an artist), trained horses in Texas, became a gardener in Alabama...

Dad's opinion of my writing and me improved none as a result of my itinerate life as a vagabond. "He's a bum," he assured Mom. "He'll end up in prison just like your brother James."

Frost bite attacked my nose and fingers on the way to New York to catch a freighter to Europe. I headed south where it was warm, and just kept heading south. In April 1965, almost exactly a year after I left Whidbey Island and Seattle, I crossed the Everglades into Miami, Florida. I had a total of eight dollars in the pocket of my well-worn jeans.

I parlayed quarters on credit at a run-down rooming house on skid row. It was called Fowler House. My dingy room (no window) was four steps across one way, eight the other. It contained the twin of a bed, an open closet of sorts, and a table on which I could write. It reminded me of author Henry Miller's description of his room in Paris.

I had to find a job—and quick. I lived on a sandwich a day for the next three weeks while I sought work. The sandwich consisted of one piece of white bread and one slice of bologna. Normally, I weighed around 165 pounds; at the end of three weeks I was down to 124 and still slipping.

Although actually starving, I was too proud to seek help. Hungry and desperate that I was, I still got up before daylight every morning and put in my time writing at the little table before I set out to answer job ads. Nothing must kill my dream. I was convinced if I kept at it every day I would eventually become successful. After all, I had read about "starving artists" who overcame everything and prevailed. I, too, through discipline and faith, would overcome.

A full-page ad in the Miami *Herald* caught my eye. Policemen were urgently needed. I could become a cop. Why not? Grace, housekeeper at Fowler House, went with me to the Salvation Army to pick out a suit for my job interview. I had never owned a suit before. Cops were conservative, Grace said, so I should dress conservative. I picked out a quiet gray suit and paid my last two dollars for it. Grace hustled up a tie and a white shirt from somewhere.

Chief of Police Walter Headley and his department heads sat around a large table in the conference room to conduct interviews. Each police candidate was given fifteen minutes to state his case. I walked in with my curly hair short-cropped (again thanks to Grace), head up, shoulders squared, feeling resplendent in my new used suit. There was a long, long silence.

Finally, someone said, "Son, where did you get that suit?"

It never occurred to me to lie. "Salvation Army, sir."

What I had purchased, unknowingly, which explains why I got it so cheap, was a 1930s-era zoot suit, complete with wide, double-breasted lapels, padded shoulders the width of a door, and baggy pleated trousers. I was in the room for an hour answering questions about my adventures. I got the job. My first police identification card gave my weight as 126 pounds and listed my build as *thin.*

As a Miami, Florida police officer. With son David.

Years later, instructors at the Miami police academy were still telling the story of the kid from skid row who showed up in a zoot suit to become a cop.

# # #

I chased criminals in Miami for the next four years. I worked vice—prostitution—and then transferred to a uniformed "salt-and-pepper" team patrolling the black ghettos. Up until this time, police departments in the South were pretty much segregated, like the rest of society. My partner was a tall black guy named Charles Daniels. We became as tight as brothers. I kept telling him that one day I was going to write a book about us. One day, as it turned out, I did.

"It's a war going on in them mean streets," a black cop named Vic Butler used to say. "The war'll kill you too if you don't watch out."

One night my partner Charles Daniels and I were pinned down in the stairwell of a ramshackle rooming house by a junkie armed with a .25 auto. He kept cracking open his door and popping off at us with his little pistol. *Pop! Pop! Pop!* Like that. Then he'd slip inside, slip in another clip, and try it again.

In between clips, we charged. The door opened a crack and the pistol thrust out at us, pointing directly at my chest. By some miracle the junkie failed to pull the trigger. He darted back inside.

Daniels blew a hole the size of a man's head through the door with his shotgun. There was an awful scream.

A moment later, the .25 appeared through the hole in the door, held by two fingers. The dude was ready to give up.

There was still screaming from inside. A woman. She had been lying up in bed drunk. One of the pellets from Daniel's buckshot round had neatly blown off her little toe.

Vic Butler shook his head when he heard of the shooting.

"I hear you almost bought the farm last night," he said. "You'd better remember what I told you if you want to live long enough to collect your medals."

"It *felt* like war," I conceded.

"It *is* war," he said.

Shortly after that, I shot off a dude's top lip. A freak shot at an armed fleeing felon who was going to shoot me. No teeth, no nose, just lip. The other cops started making bets on which part of the human anatomy Daniels or I would get next. *Homicide!* (Pocket Books, 1990)

The Vietnam War, which had been little more than a whisper, a rumor, while I was in the navy, began heating up. I enlisted in the U.S. Army Reserves and went active duty for training, becoming a Special Forces (Green Beret) weapons expert. I ran one across-the-border mission into Laos to intercept and booby-trap a Ho Chi Minh Trail by which the North Vietnamese sent troops and war supplies south. I would return to Vietnam in 1983 to run clandestine missions with Ho *Co* Minh, who attempted to recruit a guerrilla army to fight the Soviets and the North Vietnamese communists after the fall of Saigon in 1975. All these experiences were to provide material and background for both novels and nonfiction books I eventually wrote.

In Vietnam. Second from left.

I also got married to a black-haired, green-eyed Jewish girl named Dianne. Our son, David, was born exactly one year later. I couldn't take my eyes off him. I thought him a miracle. I lugged him around everywhere I went.

Dianne and I first lived in an apartment in Hialeah, moved to a duplex in Miami after David was born, and finally ended up in a bungalow in North Miami. Wherever we lived, as it had always been, there was a desk in some corner where I got up every day to write. Every day I wrote, no matter what else happened.

I sold few pieces; those I did sell garnered very paltry sums indeed. Somehow Dianne seemed threatened by my devotion to writing. She never understood why I kept banging my head against the stone. More than once she asked me why I even bothered.

"I'm going to be a writer," I assured her.

She didn't want to talk about it. It was almost like I was hiding something shameful—like hard-core porn or a secret addiction. So I didn't talk about it. I just kept writing. I wrote when I received nothing but rejection slips, hundreds of them. I wrote when my heart was heavy as well as when I had great joy. I *wrote.*

I was going to become a *writer.*

# CHAPTER THREE

Even when I wasn't publishing much, writing provided an enormous sense of fulfillment. Success in writing, I kept telling myself, didn't happen overnight. It was measured in years of hard work. I devoted the time; I was committed to the process. All I had to do was show up every day and write. Each day that I wrote I felt myself moving another step nearer my goals. I knew I was getting better. I received more acceptances, more checks. Dianne called my work an "obsession."

An acquaintance sighed and shook his head. "I always wanted to become a writer," he said.

"Yeah? Why aren't you?"

"I had this great idea for a book. They rejected me, so I gave up."

Most wannabe writers give up. They haven't the discipline and the perseverance to keep at it. If writing were easy, *everybody* would be a writer. Successful writers never give up, no matter what.

By 1978 I was a police homicide detective in Tulsa, Oklahoma. Dianne and I had been married over twelve years. We had two sons, David and Michael. I was working seven jobs: cop; director of the Criminal Justice Program at American Christian College; instructor at Tulsa Junior College; shoplifting detective for Safeway Stores; security guard at St. Francis Hospital; a member of the U.S. Army Special Forces Reserves; writer. I was also attempting to build a horse ranch near Mannford, 35 miles west of Tulsa. My average work day, seven days a week, began at four a.m. when I got up to write and ended about midnight.

Dianne was a stay-at-home mom. She liked it. I worked extra jobs so we could afford for her to be at home with our sons, rather than their being raised by Day Care and baby sitters. No matter how hard I worked, however, it never seemed to be enough. I heard Dianne remarked to friends, "I've always had champagne tastes on a beer budget."

31

I felt like I was the beer budget. I was exhausted all the time. Dianne's solution was for me to give up writing, which produced little income anyhow. "You could get two extra hours of sleep," she said.

Investigating a murder as a Tulsa homicide detective.

By this time I had been a cop and out in the streets working nothing but high crime for some thirteen years. Four in Miami, almost nine in Tulsa, the only break being a little over a year I took off to earn a bachelor's degree at Florida State University in Tallahassee. I had been stabbed once and shot at a number of times. I killed a sniper in a gunfight during the rioting that accompanied the 1968 Republican National Convention in Miami. As a homicide detective, I lived every day with violence and death. I felt it rotting out my soul. No one can walk constantly through the sewers of humanity without being affected. The job was actually destroying me. I built up emotional walls.

One day I went to Dianne. "I can't do this anymore," I said.

"You can teach," she said, looking worried.

"I don't want to teach. I want to become a full-time freelance writer."

My first novel, *No Gentle Streets*, had been accepted by a small New York publishing house. I was regularly publishing magazine articles and bringing in about $300 a month selling to the true detective magazines. If I devoted full-time to writing, with the discipline I had developed over the years, I knew I could make a living at it. Hadn't I always provided?

Dianne had little faith. Obviously, the money, the security, was more important to her than my well-being or my ambitions. She looked at me as though I had gone mad. Her first response was, "How much money can you make?"

Not long afterwards, she got up early and came into the tiny room where I wrote of mornings before I went on-duty at the police station. "I want a divorce," she said.

I had to sell the ranch. I gave everything to Dianne; after all, it was my fault that I wanted to be a writer. She took the new car, the furniture, money from selling our property, and the boys and moved back to Florida. I was left with my books and a quarter horse stallion named Storm. I moved in with my brother Joe in Tulsa, so depressed that the police department took me temporarily out of homicide and sent me to the "rubber gun squad." Losing my sons, having them taken fifteen hundred miles away where I could not be a part of their lives, would plague me forever.

We were prospecting for gold, my old army buddy and I, in the Superstitions of Arizona. At least, that was the excuse we gave for being in that wasteland, the remotest piece of real estate on the continent. Actually, we were running away, both of us...

So here we were, plodding along with our backpacks as the sun beat down like an old stove-heated flatiron and the temperature pushed 120 degrees. Here we were, hiding from everything and everybody. From man, whom we no longer trusted, and from God, in Whom we no longer believed...

"Lost In The Superstitions," *Guideposts*

I survived the only way I knew how—by writing. Retreating to my lonely circle of light. Escaping from the turmoil in my heart and soul. Writing the way I had since I was seven years old at the makeshift desk Mom built for me in that "ticky place" shack in the woods.

Bitter and angry, I stuck it out with the police for another year. One night I chased a fleeing fugitive on foot into an alley at Third Street and Utica. It was after midnight and the streets were largely abandoned. I clutched my .357 revolver in my fist as, boiling with rage, I chased this scumbag down the alley and cornered him against a building. We faced off, both of us panting from the fast, hard chase. The guy was a tall black man with bulging muscles and defiance written all over his face. We were one on one in a dark alley.

"You puke-white honky muthafucka," he snarled, and spat a gob that splattered on my shirt front. "I be walkin' out a'here over the top'a your white ass."

I felt a coolness in the pit of my stomach, like a sudden temperature lowering. I even smiled as I took a step forward, slowly lifted my revolver, and pointed it at the bridge of the man's nose. The revolver remained steady. I was still smiling.

I said, "You won't be walking out of here at all."

"You won't be shootin' none'a me, muthafucka." He didn't sound quite as cocksure of himself.

There was no one else around, just him and me. I slowly pressured the trigger. The hammer started back.

"What you think you doin', muthafucka?"

All I had to do was testify that he, a wanted felon, resisted arrest. I kept smiling.

The dude's eyes popped wide. They cast back the distant yellow glare from a streetlight. I picked out exactly where I wanted the bullet to go. *This* lowlife maggot would victimize no further innocents.

"Good night, cocksucker," I said, "...and goodbye."

The hammer started to break and fall. Only my own voice speaking, clear and loud suddenly in the night, stopped it. I had always promised myself I would never let the sewage from the streets penetrate my tough cop's skin to reach me personally. Now, here I was—a homicide detective about to commit homicide. I caught people for this and put them in prison.

My cop's skin was gone, worn away by personal tragedy and years in the streets.

Scorn returned to the fugitive's face when he saw my gun hand start to tremble. "Honky, I be goin' right over your stinkin' ass like a dose'a salts."

The man would never know how close he came to being dead. I eased down the hammer on the revolver. It was still an effort to keep from going through with it. I was trembling all over.

The dude advanced. I reached as far back as I could with the heavy weapon. It split the air in a shrill whistle as I brought it around with all the strength I could put into it. I felt the barrel bury itself into skin and flesh and bone. The guy dropped unconscious to the ground like an empty sack.

I turned in my resignation the next day. I was 37-years-old. I was going to step into that difficult arena to become a full-time freelance writer. Now I'd see if those many years of discipline would carry me through.

# CHAPTER FOUR

According to a survey, the thing people most want to do that they're not doing now is write a book. They look upon writing as glamorous and lucrative. They think all they have to do is apply themselves. I've often heard people say they'll "retire and write" one of these days, or that they'll write a book if their professional endeavor of the moment doesn't pan out. Unfortunately, writing is one of the few fields where merely *wanting to* doesn't mean much.

```
We regret to inform you that after
careful consideration we have decided
your submission does not meet our cur-
rent editorial needs. The Editors
```

What could be more discouraging than an impersonal, anonymous, unsigned, printed rejection form? I could almost barf when I looked in the mirror and recognized the naked lust to succeed in my eyes. You're a phony, I told myself. Give it up. Stop wasting your time. Quit.

Andrew Dubus wrote, "I think most writers quit between the ages of twenty and thirty, for various reasons... They don't have friends who really understand what they are doing. They don't get published; they work and work and don't get any money for it. There is no one who cares whether they work, no one who can threaten them with firing, no one to set the alarm clock for..."

I understood all this, how hard it was going to be, how hard it had already been. Still, I assured myself that everything looked impossible to the people who never tried anything—and I quit the Tulsa police department on April 16, 1979.

I had not been idle during the year since Dianne divorced me. I saved some money and bought five acres of unimproved scrubland near the Illinois River in northeastern Oklahoma. It was so far back in the woods, as the old saying goes, that even sunlight had to be piped in. On the weekend before I left the police, I went out to the land and constructed out of plyboard and

36

two-by-fours an 8x16-foot building which promptly came to be known as "the tool shed." Nearby, I erected a two-holer out-house. I felt right uptown.

"I'm going to quit being a cop and write," I informed my girlfriend Kathy. "You can either stay in Tulsa—or you can come with me."

It wasn't like I didn't warn her in advance. She had a choice. I was nothing if not a romantic.

As a professional rodeo bronc rider. This photo appeared in *Rodeo Sports News*.

Kathy as 23-years-old and divorced with a two-year-old son, Joshua. She was blond, blue-eyed, sexy and gorgeous. Not exceptionally bright—but with her legs she didn't have to be. We were married and moved into the tool shed, accompanied by admonishments from her family to "divorce that fool." We intended to live in the tool shed while I built a "real house" in the clearing.

The shed was big enough for a regular bed across one end and Joshua's smaller bed below the single Plexiglas window. At the other end I moved in a desk. Most of my books were stored at my brother's house. The kitchen consisted of a Coleman camp stove. A kerosene lamp supplied light; there was no electricity.

I built a fence for my stallion Storm, a pen to hold some chickens for eggs and drumsticks, and a truck patch in which to grow vegetables. I bought a baby milk goat we named Izzy and some ducks. We'd get a pig next year and maybe a beef. The "back to the land" movement was huge in the United States at the time.

We quickly settled into a routine. Early every morning, as always over the years, I got up to put in my hours writing. I was generally through by noon. A quick lunch, followed by an hour or so of working in the vegetable garden, and then I directed my labors toward building the real house. It was going to be small, only 600 square feet, consisting of a living room and attached kitchen, two bedrooms and a tiny "library" where I would keep my desk and books. Where, I reassured Kathy, I would work and become famous. Upon which time we would have a much larger *real* house.

I built the house with hand tools since there was no electricity. Hammering and sawing and pouring concrete and roofing far into the night by light supplied from kerosene lanterns. We'd go to bed, get up before daylight the next morning so I could write my six hours, then back to raising the house.

It was hard work, but it was a wonderful summer. In the hot afternoons, the three of us piled on Storm's bare back and rode down to the river for a swim. Often after nightfall, other "homesteading" friends dropped by and we built a fire and sat around it underneath the stars telling stories. Kathy, Joshua and I were brown, healthy and happy.

*No Gentle Streets*, my novel about homicide cops, still hadn't been released. I was working on another novel and a nonfiction book while also casting out a dozen or more articles and short stories every month. I received rejection slips, lots of them. Fortunately, I had previously cultivated a couple of regular paying markets that kept us minimally supplied, the most lucrative of which was the true detective magazine fields. Two separate companies published a total of eight different monthlies. I always had two or three crime articles in the mags each month to stave off starvation.

James Michener once observed that if he were a young man again, "I would not hesitate at writing anything to get into print, except pornography."

"I'm a prostitute," I said. "I'll write for anybody who'll pay me."

I discovered under the *Men's* section of *Writer's Market* a promising-sounding market for action-adventure short stories. *Gent*, the entry said, was similar to *Gentlemen's Quarterly* or *Esquire* and paid $200 for 2,000-word stories. Hemingway had never made that kind of money per word. I pounded out a couple of Vietnam war stories based on combat experiences in Special Forces. I received checks for them and waited for the first one to come out.

Neither convenience stores nor bookstores displayed copies of *Gent*. I was advised to go to an adult bookstore. It turned out *Gent* had a subtitle: *Home of The D-Cups*. Ray porn. Not only that, but the pictures were of fat, sloppy women with acne and enormous udders that flopped down past their navels. No style at all.

Sure enough though, right in the middle of all that flesh was my byline. Charles W. Sasser. Worse yet, another story with my byline was coming out next month. What would my friends say?

I needn't have worried. Even if my friends happened to see it, they weren't apt to admit it. Sorry about the pornography, Michener.

Author and columnist Jay Cronley was right when he commented in one of his columns that "nobody on his own could survive in much style as a freelance magazine writer." The operative phrase here is "in much style." I wrote literally hundreds of articles directed at every conceivable magazine. A check miraculously appeared in the mailbox every time our coffer got down to five or six dollars between us and the next meal. We might not have lived in style, as Cronley warned, but our needs and wants for the time being were simple and we survived. Articles I wrote about life in the tool shed actually paid for the materials needed to construct the real house.

We built our new house in the meadow during a single day. I drove the last nail well before sundown. My wife was busy keeping two-year-old Joshua's hands out of the paint bucket. She ran out of green paint and finished the back and one side in melon.

I had to grin as I stepped back to admire our work. "At least," I said, "it belongs to us. No thirty-year mortgage on that masterpiece of modern architecture."

Kathy's answering smile was wistful. "It's small," was all she said before flying inside to turn an eight-by-sixteen foot tool shed into a home...

"Taming The Tool Shed," *Farmstead*

At midnight I awoke to the worst thunder and lightning I'd ever heard or seen. For a few seconds I lay in bed, and then watched as the shed roof above me tore off and blew away. I ran outside without bother to dress. The unfinished house looked as if it were about to go. The roof shuddered; studs hummed like harp strings, the wind threatening to pluck them right out of their new braces.

The next thing I knew I was on the roof. The house shook in the storm's jaws like an old shoe in a terrier's. Strobe lightning outlined the skeletal frame. I scurried around crablike in the wind and slashing rain, pounding nails into the roof, trying to get it to hold, trying to preserve the house by sheer force of will.

"God, we need this new start!" I prayed, but the violent night whipped the prayer to shreds. I screamed, "God I can't let You destroy it! I can't let You!"

"Here Is Where We'll Build Our House," *Guideposts*

# # #

Kathy, Joshua and I moved into the real house before the snow flew. We had electricity, propane heat, indoor water and plumbing, and an office-library for me. I brought all my books out of storage.

The skills I acquired with cameras while serving as a reporter in the navy contributed considerably to my marketability as a journalist during this period of magazine writing. In the army we called it a "force multiplier." As a "participatory journalist," I soon earned a reputation for writing about the offbeat and the adventurous. I traveled a lot during those years, sometimes taking Kathy and Joshua with me where there was no danger involved. By the time Joshua was four years old he would tap me on the head with one finger and burst into the Willie Nelson song *"On the road again..."*

Before a performance (left) as a rodeo clown and bullfighter, with partner Gerald Barnhart.

We rode "chicken buses" all over Mexico, hiked Padre Island, chased wild mustangs in Nevada, canoed the Suwannee River... I become a professional rodeo clown and bullfighter, volunteered for a year's active duty training as a medic with U.S. Army Special Forces... I cranked out magazine articles for *Wild West; The Ozark Mountaineer; Oklahoma Living; Christian Life; Rider; Home Life; Guideposts; Animals; Guns & Ammo; American Survival Guide; Byline; Fur-Fish-Game; Lost Treasure...*

A tug pushing a series of domino-like barges upriver bucked and yawed in the stronger current where the mighty Mississippi narrowed to let itself be spanned by the bridge connecting Port Pleasant, Arkansas, and Greenville, Mississippi. If the river could do that to a tug, I reflected, what might it do to the postage-sized raft of Styrofoam and plyboard we had just launched?

"Huck Finning The Mississippi," *High Adventure*

Some of the best lobstering appears to be offshore of the mangrove islands and clumps where the sandy bottom tapers down into rocky ledges and the water is ten to twenty feet deep. Of course, lobsters abound in deeper water, but snorkel diving to depths of twenty feet can be exhausting...

"Diving For Bugs," *Florida Keys*

The 1980s was the heyday of the paramilitary magazines. Shelves were stocked with *Soldier of Fortune; New Breed; Eagle; Modern Warfare; Survive; Vietnam Combat... Soldier of Fortune* was still a black-and-white rag when I sold my first piece to editor Bob Brown, a Special Forces vet; I received $50 for it. By the 1980s I was selling him pieces for up to $1,000. that kind of payments made it worthwhile going to war.

For ten years, all through the 1980s and up through *Desert Storm* in 1991, the first war in Iraq, it was a standing joke among my friends that if there was a war somewhere, Chuck Sasser was probably there. I made a decent living as a freelance combat correspondent writing for the paramilitaries, as a stringer for Tulsa *Tribune*, and eventually by writing sections of books on modern warfare for *Time/Life*. I roamed the jungles with the *contras* in Nicaragua, patrolled with the Salvadorans, edged back into Vietnam with the National United Front For The Liberation of Vietnam (NUFLVN)... It got hairy sometimes. I was shot on the Honduran border and involved in several savage firefights. Often, I volunteered for active duty with the Green Berets when it appeared a good mission was coming down the pipe. I parachuted into Panama and onto the Korean DMZ...

> It was into this dangerous land just south of the DMZ that combined U.S.-Korean SF (Special Forces) troops would be inserting by parachute... My own counterpart was a lieutenant named Lee Shik. We jumped together from a Korean C-130 onto a sandbar in the Little Han River. The C-130 did not fly well and seemed in need of repairs.
>
> From the air we could see the wide slash of the DMZ. Lee pointed it out to me.
>
> "The communists have FROG missiles," he said when we were on the ground. "The range of the FROG is 70 kilometers. It can hit Seoul. Seoul is only 40 kilometers away. Our country is always under the FROG."
>
> "Korea Waits For War," *Soldier of Fortune*

Jim Morris, my editor and friend at *Eagle* magazine, transferred over to Dell Publishing Company as military editor, a move that led to my finally acquiring a literary agent. Jim planned to publish a series of books at Dell on different military units. He wanted me to write the volume on the Green Berets. Up to this time, the only book I had published was the police novel *No Gentle Streets*. Although it received great reviews from *Library Journal, Publisher's Weekly* and *Mostly Murder*, I made much more money writing for the paramilitaries.

A newly-formed literary agency headed by Ethan Ellenberg handled the procurement of writers for Jim's project. Ethan wrote me a letter, since I still refused to have a telephone. Naturally, I leapt at Jim's offer. The project, however, fell through. Ethan wrote me another letter in which he offered to represent me as my agent. By this time I had been freelancing full-time for some five years and had not once attempted to acquire an agent.

Flying on a mission with U.S. Army Special Forces (center). With team leader Lieutenant Steve Ecker (left) and team engineer Sergeant Alan Bodine.

That's one of the Catch-22s in this business. When you need an agent, you can't find one. When you don't think you need one, there they are.

I fired Ethan a letter right back. "Why should I give you ten percent of what I make?" I demanded. "Where were you when I *really* needed you?"

Ethan patiently explained an agent's duties and the advantages of having one. We have now been friends and business associates for some twenty years. He was certainly right about the advantages.

Today, a professional, I have come a long way from when I was a kid in the "ticky place" shack, and from the tool shed, but I find discipline is a requirement that has never changed. It is as important in my career today as it was when I was a wannabe writing what no one seemed to want to read. Every working day, religiously, I put in my hours as though I were drawing a salary, as though a stern boss were looking over my shoulder.

"You really are dependable, a pleasant change," e-mailed Bill Fawcett, a book packager and author for whom I have written several novels.

Being dependable is essential in the writing business. Dependability derives from discipline. While the skills of writing can be learned and the love of words and books is granted or you wouldn't *want* to be a writer, the most important ingredient you can possess for success is *discipline*. I can unequivocally promise you one thing: Without discipline you will *never* become a writer.

Parachuting with U.S. Army Special Forces (foreground).

# SECTION II:
# Inspiration

*"Good work doesn't happen with inspiration. It comes from constant, often tedious, and deliberate effort. If your vision of a writer involved sitting in a café, sipping an aperitif with one's fellow geniuses, become a drunk. It's easier and far less exhausting."*

— *William Hefferman*

Hopping freights gathering materials for articles on the
"homeless"

# CHAPTER FIVE

Writing is one of the few professions in which you can bang your poor sore head on the desk every day for years with no certainty that your efforts will ever pay off with a check. War begins every time you sit down in your lonely circle of light, no matter how long you have been in the business. Self-doubt forms ranks against confidence and barrages it with mortar rounds. Despair sneaks in through the jungle and ambushes faith. Procrastination conducts psyops (psychological operations) against discipline. Raw reality launches raids against your dream.

Then why would *anybody* want to be a writer? Before discussing inspiration as it applies to *what* to write and *how* to write it, perhaps we should first consider the question of *why* we write. From where does such inspiration come in the first place?

I teach one writing course each year at Tulsa Community College; any more than that and I become a teacher, not a writer. I often ask my students the *why* question. Why do you want to be a writer? I receive a variety of answers, starting with philosophical reasons: Self-expression, communication; to change the world... Other responses are more practical: Fame; prestige; money; self-employment; travel; adventure; to be in charge of one's own life...

One student didn't want to *write*; he wanted to *be* a writer. He stared at me for a long moment, trying to think of an answer. Finally, he blurted out, "I don't like to read, but I still want to be a writer and change the world. I thought you could tell me how."

If you want to change the world, give up writing and go out and join the Peace Corps. Although writers do, in fact, possess influence, sometimes out of all proportion to their intellectual qualifications, changing the world is not a legitimate prime mover for wanting to become a writer. That motivation and a couple of dollars you earned at a *real* job will get you a cup of java at Starbuck's.

I thought of a college writing class Flannery O'Connor once taught in which he remarked, "Everywhere I go I'm asked if I think universities stifle writers. My opinion is that they don't stifle enough of them."

I also ask my students the question: When was the last time you wrote? Last week? Three weeks ago? Six months? Not good enough. Writers *write*. They don't grab a beer and flake out in front of the boob tube waiting for inspiration to strike like a bolt of lightning out of the blue.

I earned less than $5,000 the first year after I resigned from the police department and moved into the tool shed. I do okay now. I have a horse ranch and a nice large house; I don't have to get up in the morning and build a fire in order to thaw the ice and snow that blew in underneath the door overnight, as I did when I was a kid. The insulation is no longer old newspapers and tar paper tacked on the walls, and I don't write at a desk made of vegetable crates and old boards.

Still, if my inspiration for becoming a writer was to get rich, I could have applied my talents and energies to a number of far more lucrative pursuits. I *could* have been rich, if that were my goal. Instead, I became a writer.

During the years after Kathy, Joshua and I moved out of the tool shed and into the "real house" on what we called The Farm, I became known in that remote, rural section of Oklahoma as "the writer." Rather like a landmark. "Go down past that dirt road where the writer lives and go on three more miles until the road intersects, turn left where there's a bunch of hay and go..." Neighbors who could read even read some of my stuff. *No Gentle Streets* finally came out in hardcover.

Each morning, I got up long before daylight to get in my writing. I took a break after sunrise to do chores—feed Storm and the chickens, ducks and goat—before I put on cut-off jeans and running shoes for a five-mile jog down winding dirt roads to the river and back. One morning, an old Mercury full of fat women pulled up alongside as I was running along.

"Are you Charles Sasser the writer?" one of them asked out the car window.

I stopped. I was dripping sweat. "Well... yes."

That was the end of the exchange. Without another word, the four hefty dames jumped out of the car with a Brownie camera and started taking pictures. They took turns posing with me. Throwing arms over my perspiring shoulders and around my waist as though we were old buddies. Like anglers posing with a good fish catch. Then they jumped back in the Mercury without so much as a by-your-leave and roared off in a cloud of dust.

I stood there in the road looking after them, stunned. That was my big moment of recognition and prestige. The vast majority of us who make our living as writers are not famous like Tom Clancy, Danielle Steel, or Stephen King. We make our living more or less in obscurity, unknown except within our immediate regions and within our own limited clutches of fans. Life has a way of humbling you when you start to think otherwise.

One of my favorite book stores is *Steve's Books & Sundries*, a privately-owned book store in Tulsa that, though jammed with books, magazines and newspapers, still makes room for a sandwich bar in the back like the old-fashioned neighborhood news stands. Steve always makes a big production of my new book releases—ads in the newspapers, signs in the front window, a table stacked with copies of my new book and past titles.

So I was sitting there with my quick-draw pen at the ready when a lady rushed up dragging her small son, who wore a pained expression and clasped the front of his jeans with both hands.

"Do you work here, sir? Where's the bathroom?"

"Go   right   through   that   door   and   turn   right—"

It's a ritual that men meeting other men ask each other the question of what they do for a living. I often reply, "I'm a plumber." Saves a lot of time and energy. If I admit to being a writer, the next question, posed with a little edge of disbelief, is, "Oh? Have you published anything?" Nobody ever asks me if I've plumbed anything.

So *why* do we become writers? Years ago when he was a young man, Jerry Lewis taught a seminar on comedy at the University of Southern California. The answer to one single question determined whether or not an applicant was admitted to the course.

"Huck Finning the Mississippi." Sons (left to right) David and Michael, with their friend David McCracken.

"Why do you want to be a comedian?" Lewis asked.

He accepted only one answer, or some variation of it: "Because I have to be. Because there's something in me nagging and torturing and demanding to get out. I absolutely have to make people laugh."

Why do you want to be a writer? Because you *have* to be. That, I believe, is the core of the writer's inspiration. Everything else—fame, prestige, money, self-expression—is nothing but byproduct. I have always thought that writing chose me instead of the other way around.

When I was a kid we used to go to town on Saturday mornings in an old wooden farm wagon pulled by a red one-eyed mule and a big black mare. Farmers parked their wagons in the back alley at Sallisaw and hung around all day selling produce and gabbing. My grandpa was a drunk. We had to pull him out of Tump Kinsey's bar and pool room at nightfall when we were ready to go home and pour him into the bed of the wagon. Returning home late at night, I lay in the wagon bed with my head resting on my grandpa and gazed up at the stars, dreaming of all the things I would do. As I told my mom, I would live many lives, not just one—and write about them.

I never questioned *why* I would be a writer. I simply accepted it as fact. It wasn't until 1985 when I became a finalist for NASA's Journalist-in-Space project, vying to be the first writer to fly the shuttle into space, that I had to confront the *why* question head-on.

A total of 1,703 journalists and writers had applied for the privilege. That number was soon reduced to 100. Walter Cronkite and I were still in the running. Eliminated so far were Geraldo Rivera, ABC White House correspondent Sam Donaldson, and NBC anchorman Tom Brokaw. Not bad company, a friend quipped, for a guy who grew up barefooted and didn't know what indoor plumbing was.

From such things were fairy tales drawn. I never dreamed that one day I might have the chance to step among the stars, that I might, in a single lifetime, go from a horse drawn wagon to a rocket hurtling through space.

Since we had no telephone, I didn't know I was a finalist until in the afternoon when a crowd of people came thronging out of the woods loaded with TV cameras and popping flashbulbs. You had to really want to find me to reach The Farm. The main highway led off into a secondary road, which became a blacktop, which turned into a dirt road, which eventually became a pair of ruts. At the end of the ruts, you parked and followed a trail up through the woods until you reached the house.

Kathy and I had decided to build native stone siding around our house. I was busy laying rock when the media descended upon me in a frenzy. All I wore were a pair of cut-off jeans and an old pair of combat boots. Dusted with cement mixed with sweat, I appeared on the networks that night dubbed as "Li'l Abner," the hillbilly who might rocket into space.

"Why do you want to go?" a member of the final selection panel asked me.

"To see," I immediately replied. "To experience. To go where so few others have gone. To be among those who take first tentative steps off this planet on journeys to put footprints on the stars. And then to write so others may experience it through me."

Taking my mother, Mary, on her first airplane flight.

The Challenger disaster of January 28, 1986, in which seven astronauts were killed, including teacher-astronaut Christa McAuliffe, ended NASA's civilian program. No journalist would fly. Although the greatest adventure of the century was not to be mine, at least not yet, I later realized that in my yearning to go into space I had also made my "mission statement" and clarified my inspiration for becoming a writer.

"To see. To experience. To go where so few others have gone... and then to write so others may experience it through me."

# CHAPTER SIX

John Steinbeck wrote most of his classic masterpiece, *Grapes Of Wrath,* at Lake Tahoe, Nevada, alone in a cabin in the woods. He would write, then get up and chop wood to clear his mind. He kept a journal that reflected what he perceived to be his lack of inspiration.

"If I can keep an honesty, it is all I can expect of my poor brain..." he chronicled. "If I can do that, it will be all my lack of genius can produce. For no one else knows my lack of ability the way I do... Sometimes, I seem to do a good little piece of work, but when it is done it slides into mediocrity ... I feel very small and inadequate and incapable."

Nonetheless, he kept at it every day until he finished. Inspiration is nothing more than simply sitting down and getting to work when there are as many reasons to give up and quit as there are to go on. I can think of no more solitary profession than being a writer."

"If you can quit," said Alexander Blackburn, former senior editor of *Writer's Forum,* "you probably should."

Whatever your inspirations for wanting to be a writer, the first thing you should do before even thinking of going cold turkey to freelance is to conduct an honest analysis of the pros and cons. You may find that, in your particular instance, the list of practical pros pales in comparison to the cons.

Lets start with the advantages of being a writer. Freelancing at home means no long commutes to work in traffic and no punching the time clock; you simply get up and walk to your desk, quite a comfort when it is snowing or raining. Working at home entails lower miscellaneous expenses, such as those for clothing, eating out, gasoline, and coffee breaks to the nearest Starbuck's. You don't have to answer to a boss when you need to go to the dentist or take Rover to the vet. You set your own work hours and are literally master of your own fate to a large extent. On top of that, you can deduct quite a number of expenses from your income tax—providing you have much income. Sometimes, large checks come in the mail.

On the other hand, the con side, you either produce or you don't eat. It is estimated that most salaried employees actually work less than five hours of each eight-hour work day. The rest of the time they're gabbing at the water fountain, playing solitaire on the PC, or gazing out the window daydreaming of being somewhere else. A writer does too much gabbing, playing solitaire or gazing out the window and large checks will *never* come in the mail. Even so, there will often be long dry spells between checks, creating a feast or famine effect.

Boxing in the U.S. Navy

Since you are self-employed, you have to pay your own health insurance and arrange your own pension plan, if you can afford it, which most writers cannot. Your social security payments to the government double, as you are both employer and employee. You never have a paid vacation or sick day. If you computer goes on a blitz or you run out of paper and pens, you have to make your own repairs and pay for your own supplies. No more calling up the company's Maintenance or Supply section. Deadlines, if you are lucky, constantly hover over your head. Friends and family feel free to interrupt at any time; after all, you aren't working since you don't have a *real* job. Finally, it can get lonely sitting at a desk by yourself so much of the time. I sometimes turn up the radio full blast for a few minutes just to hear human voices.

If you aren't already discouraged, let me add that your personal relationships will suffer. This may be the profession's greatest disadvantage. No writer is truthful who does not tell you of the sacrifices he makes and the sacrifices those around him must make. Loving a writer in the long term, especially in the beginning of his career, is frankly beyond the capability and patience of most people.

Each writer or potential writer should come equipped with a government warning tab attached like those on mattresses, the removal of which is a violation of law. Before a writer marries, before he even has a first date, he should require a prospective mate to fill out a detailed application concerning temperament and nature and understanding. There are so few of us that most people you meet will never have met a *real* writer. It takes a special person to understand and to accept a writer's dreams, drive and ambitions. I was 53-years-old before I met a woman like that.

Writing—my dreams of it, the inspiration that motivated my life—generated a regretful amount of heartache.

Dianne divorced me partly because I wanted to *be* a writer. She took my sons 1500 miles away. I wrote them letters and never received replies; it turned out she kept the letters and never let the boys read them. I telephoned and was told they didn't want to talk to me. I begged her to let them spend summers with me.

"They don't want to see you," Dianne said. "They don't want to come and live like you do out in the woods."

"We have a *real* house now," I protested. "We only lived in the tool shed while we built the house."

"Maybe David and Michael will want to talk to you when you finally give up and get a job like normal men."

Dianne divorced me because I wanted to be a writer. Kathy finally divorced me because I *was* a writer. After seven years of marriage, seven years into my career as a full-time freelancer, things seemed to be heading to the top. I was earning a fairly decent living writing primarily war stuff for the paramilitaries and true crime stories. I was paying for Kathy to go to college and encouraging her to be the professional photographer she wanted to be. We were thinking of building a bigger and better house.

Kathy was a nervous, pessimistic young woman. It frightened her into depression when the Challenger space shuttle blew up as it was being launched and it seemed I might have a chance to rocket into space as a journalist. My covering wars around the globe kept her in a constant state of agitation, no matter how I tried to reassure her. I was gone part of the time, two or three weeks here and there, not much more than other men with traveling occupations. I always attempted to shield her from knowing about the hazards of combat writing.

The recon patrol was wasted, punched out, climbing the high country of Chalatenango along El Salvador's border with Honduras, trying to scare up some intelligence on the guerrillas who occupied this no-man's land. Camera equipment bag riding heavy in my pack, I had joined the government's patrol in Las Palmas to gather material for magazine articles and maybe, someday, a novel on the Salvadoran civil war. And just *experiencing* it, too, looking at this thing of war...

We cut down off the side of a mountain and entered a jungle at the bottom of a draw. A cattle trail or goat path or whatever followed the floor of the draw. The draw became a canyon that gradually narrowed between high sheer walls. The patrol waded into a clear stream. We splashed our hot faces and dunked our heads before saddling up again and moving on...

Funny. It happened just as it happens in an auto accident. One moment you're doing sixty down the expressway and the next a Peterbilt crosses the centerline roaring directly toward you. The canyon simply exploded with automatic rifle and machine-gun fire. I recall thinking how the *bark-bark* of the Soviet Kalashnikovs were deeper-throated, more guttural, than the tiny *bang-bang* of the American M16s.

I thought the world had blown up in my face.

Then it slowed down to quarter speed. It almost stopped. The scream that pierced the first thick rumble-rattle of gunfire seemed to come out of the center of the cosmos, the primal scream, and it pierced through eternity. An eternity was how long it took the radioman to fall to earth. A bullet from the first bursts had caught him in the eye. Pink mist and the scream exploded from his skull. Vasconcelos's dark face, written exaggerated with terror, turned toward him; and the pink mist sprayed his face like paint from a high-pressure can. Vasconcelos's own scream shredded the wind. He sounded like a gull in a hurricane whose cry had been ripped from his throat...

*Always A Warrior* (Pocket Books, 1994)

The breaking point with Kathy finally came when a friend of mine was killed in El Salvador. Colonel Rafael Cienfuegos was head of a Salvadoran army office called COMPREFA, a Spanish acronym that meant the armed forces press corps.

"You and me, Cholla," Cienfuegos said. *Cholla*, a type of cactus with sharp spikes, was his name for me. "You and me, Cholla, we are warriors in wars without end. For us, I fear, there can be only one end."

Cienfuegos had arranged for me to work with Colonel Ochoa, commander of the Fourth Brigade at El Paraiso. Run a few patrols. Check out the action for some magazine pieces I planned to write. I wouldn't find out about Rafael until I returned to the capital.

He had been resting on a bench at the tennis courts between sets when two terrorists walked up behind him. One of them pressed the muzzle of a .32-caliber pistol to the back of his head and squeezed the trigger. Brains and blood splattered all over the court. He was the highest-ranking officer slain in the long civil war.

With a truck rocketed by Sandinistas along *El Camino de Los Muertos* in Honduras. I was wounded in a firefight later that night.

The assistant press attaché at the American embassy had formerly been a reporter for the Tulsa *Tribune*, for which paper I was working as a Central American stringer. He knew that I was in El Salvador and that I played tennis with Cienfuegos whenever I was in-country. Although I was actually out of the city and up in the mountains with Fourth Brigade, word reached Stateside that I was with the Colonel when he was assassinated. Everyone presumed the guerrillas kidnapped me. I was reported missing.

Kathy almost had a nervous breakdown before I showed up again. I didn't know I was missing. Kathy divorced me shortly thereafter, seven weeks after I legally adopted Joshua. I relinquished house, land, everything to Kathy, as I had before to Dianne. It was easier for me to start over with nothing than it was for her. Maybe I even felt a little guilty.

Working as a combat correspondent in Central America.

"How would you like to be married to you and have to try to keep up?" asked my Special Forces buddy, Mad Dog Carson. "She should have left you a long time ago."

I moved into a condo in Tulsa. Dianne, who re-married, died of cancer when she was 42-years-old. By then I had published a number of books and was becoming fairly successful. To her credit, she telephoned me, crying, before she died and apologized for having left me and robbed me of my sons. She begged for forgiveness.

"I was so wrong," she sobbed. "I was selfish and wrong for leaving you and for taking the boys away. Chuck, I've always loved you. God forgive me."

She died four days later. I went to her funeral in Miami. To my discredit, I hardly recognized my own sons. David was in college, soon to go on to Duke University to medical school to become a doctor. Michael became a freelance writer/journalist. He and I have written two books together.

> The fire created its own wind, sucking in surrounding oxygen with the velocity of a small gale. An empty Pepsi can rattled down the street and was sucked into the fire.
> "My wife! My wife's in there! Help her!" rose a plaintive cry...
> *Last American Heroes* (with Michael Sasser, Pocket Books, 1994)

During low points in my life, I tend to return to places out of my past in order to collect my thoughts and reflect on how it all began. The next time I went out to The Farm, Kathy had sold out and moved and the *real* house in the meadow had burned down. Nothing remained in the ashes except charred lumber and piles of native sandstone with which I had labored to erect siding for the house. The tool shed was rotting down.

It was a cloudy day, as gray as my soul. I stood in the weeds where the lawn had been and took a last long look at where I

started my career as a full-time freelance writer. Then I turned
and walked slowly away. I never looked back.

In addition to considering the pros and cons of becoming a
writer, a would-be freelancer must honestly assess his own temperament. If you don't work well in solitude, if you can't take
financial and personal uncertainty, and if you buckle under ad-
versity, rejection or pressure, chances are you won't survive—no
matter your discipline and your inspiration. So why do we do it
in spite of everything?

It's because we *can't* quit. Why can't we quit? It's because
we're writers. I wouldn't want it any other way. I couldn't have
it any other way. And what is a writer?

"A writer is one who writes," said Gordon Weaver, author of
*The Eight Corners Of The World.* "A serious writer is one who
writes as well as he can as consistently as possible and for whom
writing is the most serious activity he knows. How much money,
fame or publication he gets—these are extra-literary factors."

Besides, the world *needs* writers. "We will always be necessary," said poet Rod McKuen. "There are few professions that
can claim that distinction."

# CHAPTER SEVEN

"But... but I *know* I want to *be* a writer. How do I get my inspiration for the writing itself? I have to be inspired before I can write."

So often, waiting for inspiration to strike is just an excuse for not doing the very difficult business of writing. I know wannabe writers who squander valuable time and energy talking about writing, studying writing, attending writers meetings and going to conferences, discussion groups and critiques. All this is fine and good, of course, and can be very beneficial, especially to novice writers. However, if it takes the place of actual writing, if it's a subconscious contrivance to postpone or avoid the hard, lonely labor of putting words on paper, then you may find yourself being a "writer" while never actually writing. Artistic inspiration is a highly overrated premise. I know people who have waited a lifetime for inspiration.

"I see the notion of talent as quite irrelevant," said Gordon Lish. "I see instead old-fashioned notions of perseverance, application, industry, assiduity, will, will, will, desire, desire, desire."

Personally, I see as even more irrelevant that notion of inspiration. Few of the great writers sat around waiting for the muse to descend in a flash of illumination. If they had, fine books such as *In Cold Blood, Hawaii*, and *As I Lay Dying* may never have seen print. Hemingway did not know he was writing a Nobel Prize winner with *The Old Man And The Sea*. He did not *know* he was inspired. Inspiration is nothing more than having an idea and setting out to capture its concept on paper.

The best inspiration, I've often said, is starvation. If you *know* you have to produce to pay the electric bill next month and buy Wheaties The Breakfast of Champions and cornbread mix, you are going to apply butt to chair and be inspired. Being a part-time writer is fine, if that is your goal, but the vast majority of writers who would be truly successful strive to eventually do it full-time.

I keep at least a five-day workweek. On my desk is a pad upon which I mark off six hours of daily work. Since I often work much more than that to meet deadlines, I award myself compensatory time. As of this writing, I have over 60 workdays of comp time built up. I intend taking a couple of weeks off this year to go on a fly-in fishing trip to Canada with my friend Darrell Turner and to attend a seminar on "The Great Conversation in Western Literature" at Hillsdale College in Michigan. I'll also go snow skiing for three or four days and take off a day now and then simply because I feel like taking a break.

However, I never take off from working unless I have comp time to burn; I always accumulate more overtime than I use.

What about writer's block? Are there never periods when I simply *cannot* write? My response is, I can't afford to have writer's block. I'm not even sure what writer's block is. One year when we were all skiing in Colorado, a friend, Renee Bodine, gave me a small block of wood painted yellow upon which was inscribed "Writer's Block."

"So you'll know what it is," she said.

I unequivocally make you another promise, as I did with the topic of discipline: If you have to wait for inspiration, you will *never* be a writer.

# # #

The road to the printed page is a real obstacle course for most of us. Many young writers are naturally filled with self-doubt. Some may be fortunate enough to attract mentors to help them over the obstacles. The majority, however, must run through the mines and clamber over the walls on their own, while spectators in the galleries take potshots. Therefore, the desire to be a writer, the inspiration behind the desire, must come from something deep and indestructible inside the writer's soul. For the most part, writers can expect to find little encouragement from the sidelines. Especially during the formative and novice years.

As a kid, I went around constantly with a paperback in my pocket, reading at every opportunity. For some reason, possibly because he could not read himself, it infuriated my dad. "Got his G...D...nose stuck in a book again," was his favorite commentary. "He'll never be worth a damn."

I never understood the correlation between reading and not being worth a damn, but I always felt I probably *should* be ashamed.

With then-girlfriend (later third wife) Nita touring Scotland by motorcycle.

Although Mom built me a desk, she never really took me seriously. How can you take seriously a seven-year-old kid with holes in the knees of his jeans and a dream as big as mine when no one else in the family had so much as completed high school?

When a "good job" meant the cresote plant because it got you out of the cotton fields?

What encouragement I received in my formative years came in subtle ways and was never intended as support for a budding writer. Instead, it was merely kindnesses extended to a poor kid with an active mind and imagination.

At a Mayan ruin in Guatemala.

I attended a one-room school house at McKey, Oklahoma, during the sixth and seventh grades. The school's man and wife teachers, Mr. and Mrs. Lowrimore, tolerated my turning a storm cellar into a theater. I wrote countless plays and persuaded, bribed or coerced other students to perform them.

Mr. Mullins was my English teacher in high school at Central, another isolated school so rural it let out classes six weeks in the fall so we could trek to the cotton fields of western Oklahoma to "pull bolls." Looking back, I realize Mr. Mullins at least suspected I was writing and selling book reports to my less-creative pals. Yet, he never said a word.

I was restless and quick, impatient at having to wait in class on those slower than I. That meant I often got into trouble. In his own self-defense, I'm sure, Mr. Mullins gave me a key to the school library. Anytime I finished my work in his class, I had standing permission to get up and go to the library. I read every book in it, including the encyclopedias. The experience expanded and cemented my love of books and reading.

In the hills north of Muldrow, Oklahoma, lived a writer named Eric Allen, the first true author I ever met. Mr. Allen, who wrote and published westerns, was somewhat of a recluse, or so it seemed to me. People said he stayed up there all by himself doing nothing except writing. I don't know if he had a wife or not. The Sequoyah County *Times* sometimes printed an article about him whenever he had a new paperback published. Mr. Mullins clipped the articles for me and brought me one of his books. I still have it, well-worn, in my library.

Eric Allen was a romantic figure in my mind. He was a *writer*; that was what I wanted to be. I was so shy and embarrassed when I finally met him that all I could manage to do was stand in my faded jeans, barefooted, twisting my hands one into the other.

"So you want to be a writer?" he said.

"Yes, sir."

"What kind of writing do you want to do?"

There were different kinds of writing? "I want... I want to write *everything.*"

He chuckled. A rather common-sounding chuckle from a rather common-looking man.

"If you want to be a writer," he said, giving me the best advice I was ever to receive, "then you have to work hard at it and write every day."

He would never know the influence he exerted over a barefooted little hill kid. He confirmed my belief that I *could* be a writer. Writing was my addiction, even more habit forming than smoking cigarettes.

"What you can do, or dream you can," Goethe wrote, "begin it. Boldness has genius, power, and magic in it."

> During the promotion of my seventh book, *Homicide!*, a radio interviewer asked me how it was possible that a poverty-stricken Oklahoma hill kid could have grown up to become a successful author and journalist. I thought about the question a moment.
>
> "Most kids today don't have the opportunities I had," I replied. "You see, I had a dream and I didn't *know* I couldn't catch it."
>
> Instead of poverty's turning me into a "victim" trapped by my environment, as it has so many of today's poor, it taught me valuable character traits which may seem old-fashioned and naïve, but which nonetheless opened up later opportunities. Growing up poor in rural Oklahoma, picking cotton, slopping hogs and sleeping three brothers to the bed—the ingredients of Horatio Alger stories—taught me to believe I could do whatever I wanted through hard work and discipline...
>
> "Dream Stealers," *Byline*

Out of those early years I developed three habits that carried me into my later career and provided the inspiration behind whatever success I have achieved. They are simple habits: I read, I write, I live.

Reading is the foundation of writing and of inspiration. I read omnivorously. I read virtually every day, like I write. I read literally *everything*. Fiction and nonfiction. War, adventure, horror, romance, science fiction. Biographies, autobiographies, self-improvement, how-to. Philosophy, spiritual, politics, sociology... My interests are broad and varied and I continue to cultivate them.

Ethan Ellenberg helpfully attempted to guide my career he first became my agent, pointing out that most successful writers carve out a niche and develop a readership within that category. Tom Clancy is thus known for military suspense, Stephen King for horror, John Grisham for lawyers, Judith Henry Wall for women's literature...

"Very few writers make it big in both fiction and nonfiction," he pointed out. "Very few writers can write everything."

He's absolutely right. Nonetheless, my response was, "Why should I be a writer if I write the same things over and over again?"

Like Ethan, I recommend that a writer choose his niche. Do as I say, not as I do. I've published everything from how to take care of a baby to how to garrote an enemy. My published books include biographies and autobiographies, true crime and true adventure, history, thrillers, sociology, science fiction, mysteries, action adventure... Recently, Ethan sent me an e-mail on an idea for a new book.

"I have a nutty idea for a book for you, but I think it can work," he wrote. "Here's my idea—how about one on shrunken heads? Yes, that's right, shrunken heads. When they were first discovered by Europeans. Which native groups shrink heads and why. How it's done. Which museums all over the world have them in their collections. How it fits into other kinds of "war trophies." First encounters by Europeans of headhunters. The last time a shrunken head was discovered. It's weird—but just your thing..."

Great idea. I'll probably do it.

I always wanted to go to college, figuring an education would boost me toward my goals of becoming a writer. I had no chance of attending right out of high school. Instead, I went to graduation commencement one night and left for the U.S. Navy the next morning. I was 27-years-old before I finally made it to Florida State University on scholarships and the GI Bill. I wasn't the normal student. I had a wife and son and another child on the way. I had served in the navy four years, in the U.S. Army Special Forces, and had been a big-city cop for another four years. I hobbled onto campus on crutches from having broken my ankle during the rioting that accompanied the Republican National Convention in Miami, where I had killed a sniper.

U.S. Army Special Forces A-Team, 12th Special Forces Group, Detachment ODA-213. (Second from left, kneeling)

I was never so disappointed in my life. It was the era of war protests, pot-smoking hippies in flower vans, snake dancers on campus, and be-ins. Having read so much and with such variety over the years, I was frankly better educated than the majority of my professors. Especially when it came to real life outside academia. You couldn't have stuffed a new idea into the minds of most of them with a pry bar. One young prof got up in class and "proved" that socio-political liberals were more intelligent than socio-political conservatives and were therefore superior people. Most instructors preferred that traditional-minded students such as war-mongering baby-killing Vietnam vets, ex-cops and others of our ilk remain silent during class discussions. A Vietnam vet friend of mine was automatically awarded a Gentleman's C in one class by promising not to contaminate the course by showing up for class sessions.

My opinions of academia and the so-called elite intelligentsia have never recovered from the experience.

> Consider the educational progress of a friend of mine I'll call Ken. He finished high school one spring, began college that fall, went on for his MA, then received his PhD without taking a break. With his brand new PhD, he became an associate professor at a state university. He began teaching the very same things he himself had only recently learned...
>
> They *go* to school, and then suddenly they begin *teaching* school. By design or by accident, like it or not, the academic environment effectively isolates its members from the rest of society...
>
> "Why Teachers Are Bores," *American School Board Journal*

I earned a degree in History and Anthropology, but if I had to choose my inspiration for writing from either academia or independent reading, there isn't even a toss-up. Reading will take the call every time.

I have already been discussing the second of my three habits—writing—and will continue to do so. This book is about it. That leaves the third habit—to *live*. I mean, truly live and well. Take life as a great feast and devour it all rather than nibbling around the edges. Immerse yourself in it. Experience life as a participant rather than as a spectator. Nothing inspires writing as completely as living a full life.

Although I have always believed that anyone afraid of dying is afraid to live, this does not mean you have to go off to wars, become a professional boxer or SCUBA dive with sharks. In fact, some writers believe the *deep life*, the life lived fully, is only a romantic notion. Novelist Nicholas Delbanso insisted that one has experienced by the age of four everything he needs to know to become a writer: love, pain, boredom, rage, fear of death.

Flannery O'Connor supports him. "If you can't make something out of a little experience," he wrote, "you probably won't be able to make it out of a lot. The writer's business is to contemplate experience, not to be merged with it."

I disagree. Emily Dickinson, whom most critics rank with Emerson, Poe and Whitman, wrote while living in virtual exclusion. Her poetry indicated she may have had to break away from the world to contemplate it from a distance before she could write about it. But what a horrible, lonely way to live!

In order to become fully human, you must *participate* in whatever environment you choose for yourself. I firmly believe writers must live deeply in the world, become fully human, before they can write about it, that it is through deep living that the inspiration and experience for writing derives. It offers countless plots and characters. Hemingway and Gertrude Stein went to Paris. Graham Greene went to Liberia. Herman Melville (*Moby Dick)* spent months at sea.

I could never have written about the horrors of war, given it immediacy and reality, without first going to war myself. In the same vein, how could I have told the deeper truth about cops in such books as *No Gentle Streets, Homicide!* and *At Large* without first having been a cop? Hemingway once advised a would-be writer to hang himself but arrange to be cut down before he died. That way he would have something to write about.

In an interview with Alexander Newbauer, who taught creative writing at The New School for Social Research, John Irving commented that, "My habits as a wrestler have given me more reliable tools as a writer than anything I 'learned' at either New Hampshire or Iowa (writer's workshops)."

I detest spectator sports for the simple reason that it appalls me to see people emotionally involved with watching others do things when they should be doing things themselves.

Instructing combat tactics and leadership in the U.S. Army.

After my dad died of cancer, Mom remarried a wonderful little man with two grown sons who were avid fans of every imaginable sport. They sat in front of a TV from spring baseball all the way through golf, tennis, billiards and whatever else until the end of Super Bowl, after which it all started again. They quoted statistics until your ears rang. They knew the names and pedigrees of virtually everyone who had ever batted, thrown or kicked a ball of any size or shape. Each weighed about 300 sofa-ripe pounds.

On the other hand, I worked out every day, ran mini-marathons, went down to the YMCA for a pick-me-up basketball game, and was a karate kickboxer. I turned professional kickboxer at age 51 and won my first match, after which I retired undefeated. I rode a bicycle everywhere when I lived in Tulsa, often peddling the five miles to Mom's house.

One afternoon, I bicycled over to Mom's and found one of my hefty stepbrothers ensconced on the sofa watching football. The ensuring conversation about players and plays and scores and other football trivia bored hell out of me. Finally, he noticed.

"You're not into sports, are you?" he observed, with no intent at irony.

I suppressed a smile. "No. I guess I'm not into sports."

I got up and rode my bicycle to Dale "Apollo" Cook's dojo for my daily karate and kickboxing workout.

Turning pro, and winning, in my first professional kickboxing match at age 51.

Inspiration for writing comes out of my life, as I believe it comes in one form or another from every writer's life. It has worked for me. Successes build upon each other and inspire further efforts. As of this writing, I have offers to write books from four different major editors. The agent for Richard Marcinko, whose *Rogue Warrior* series have all been New York *Times* bestsellers, solicited me for the third time to take over writing the novels. Can you believe I've turned down that kind of money and prestige?

Jon Ford, editor at Paladin Press, one of my publishers, provided in an e-mail a delightful example of the type of inspiration all writers seek.

"It's a pleasure working with an experienced author," he wrote.

Spear fishing in Mexico off Cedros Island while studying diets of sea lions.

# CHAPTER EIGHT

A blank piece of paper, said Sidney Sheldon, is God's way of telling us how hard it is to be God. That being so, doesn't a time ever come when you have to face reality, when you have to admit failure? Doesn't there come a time when you run out of inspiration, or energy, or juice, or whatever you want to call it?

I can't tell you when that times comes—or even *if* it comes. I can tell you only that not once since I was seven-years-old writing by lamplight in the "ticky place" shack have I seriously thought of giving up. It isn't that I have more willpower or inspiration than others; it has often been observed, tongue in cheek, that the secret to my success lay in the fact that I didn't have sense enough to quit. I look at it another way: I *would* be a writer, no matter what it took. I visualized my success; I daydreamed it. More importantly, I worked at it. Writing to me was something like what I described in an article I published when I was a rodeo clown bullfighter.

> One night during a lull in the action Gerald (my partner) was telling a joke about a bull being Mexican since it looked like it had sat down in guacamole. About that time the bull exploded into the arena. There was a wreck and the bull jumped into the middle of the hapless rider.
>
> Gerald made his pass. I made my pass. I could smell the bull as he got off the cowboy and began passing back at the clowns. I was going to grab his tail. Later, it dawned on me.
>
> Say you grab a 1,500-pound bull by the tail, what do you do with him then.
>
> "Rodeo Clown A Key Figure," *Oklahoma Rural News*

Writing is a 1,500-pound bull. I have it by the tail and I can't let go, won't let go.

What kills writers and their inspiration is rejection by editors, the derision of friends and family for daring to have such a preposterous dream, and the fear, in fact the sheer terror, of failure.

These are what destroy most writers even before they have careers.

I fail to understand why struggling writers collect rejection slips, those negative missiles that constantly bombard any inspiration you may retain and remind you over and over of your failures. A friend of mine thumb-tacked them to a large bulletin board above his desk. What did he see every time he glanced up? Rejection. Failure staring back at him. If you want to use the bulletin board, I scolded him, put on it copies of checks and acceptance letters. Or hang inspiring quotes. Anything, as long as it inspires and is not a depressing sign of failure. It's hard enough being a writer without looking directly at rejection every time you sit down at your desk.

When poet Jack Myers (*As Long As You're Happy*) was 27-years-old and struggling, he decided, as he put it, to "defy the main thrust of editorial opinion by literally wallpapering my study with hundreds of rejection slips. I laughed and challenged the censorious atmosphere for a month or so..."

He couldn't take it any longer. He was struck by the "depressing futility of it all. I seemed to have made a décor of failure more sturdy than my Pollyanna will to succeed. Soon I took the slips down, saved them in a box, transferred them to a larger box, threw it all out."

Good man. He should have done that in the first place.

I still get rejections. So do John Irving, Dean Koontz and Jackie Collins, although theirs may be more chummy than mine. I wad them up without reading them and try for a three-pointer in the waste paper basket. I don't need some form letter telling me my submission does not meet someone's current needs. I'll try somewhere else until I receive a check.

A writer needs to seek and cultivate positive reinforcement from friends and associates and overlook, ignore, or discard all that is destructive and not constructive. When my journalist friend Ken in the navy made his remarks about my lack of talent, I simply smiled at him and thought to myself, *Okay, we'll see.* Every time I publish a new book I send a press release to the Sequoyah County *Times*, what I consider my home town paper and the weekly that first paid me for writing. It's perverse of me, I know, but I want everyone who made fun of my dream when I was a raggedy kid to know that I made it come true.

Solo-canoeing across the Yukon.

Of course, I'm not always the optimist, not always filled with inspiration. There have been times when life wore me down and

I felt so hollow that even writing was a burden. Still, it is the act of writing that always brings me through. It has been the one thing I depend on.

With the exception of one brief interlude, I remained single for ten years after Kathy had her breakdown and left. She got married several more times and finally ended up 60 pounds overweight and on welfare. During that time, I cut a wide romantic swath through womankind. It isn't something I'm proud of, it's merely fact. Hadn't experience proved to me that writers cannot be happily married? Keep on loving 'em and keep on leaving 'em. That was my motto. No more ties that bind.

In uniform. I served 29 years in the military, active duty and reserve, and went to six wars.

By 1991 I was a reasonably successful writer. I was traveling, living well, had a pretty girlfriend, and was making more money writing than I thought possible. *Time/Life* had commissioned me to write a piece each month for a book series called *The New Face Of War*. I wrote "Winged Mounts For The U.S. Cavalry" for *Sky Soldiers* and "An Auspicious Comeback In Panama" for *Commando Operations*. I was receiving $4,000 *a month* for these pieces, on top of whatever I earned on books and magazine articles. I bought myself a sports car and some new clothes. Were Dad still alive, he would have called it living high off the hog and would have been astounded that I wasn't the bum he always thought I would become.

I had remained in the U.S. Army Reserves all these years. I was suddenly activated for military service and sent overseas for *Desert Storm*, the first war against Iraq, as First Sergeant for the 433d Military Police Company. Some other lucky scribbler finished my contract with *Time/Life*.

The ground war ended in 100 hours. For the remainder of nearly seven months' active duty I led my MP company on a law-and-order mission in Germany. The company commander was a young black captain from New Orleans, Gregory Powell. We became close friends. I proposed to my own girlfriend when he decided to bring his pregnant fiancé Monique to Europe to get married before she gave birth. We were going to have a double wedding.

Nita was a nurse, French, with black hair and gorgeous green eyes. I did love her—so why not get married? The four of us— Powell and Monique, Nita and I—caught a train from Germany to Denmark.

We married in Denmark when the cherry trees were blossoming. The four of us clasped hands, laughing and hugging each other. It rained a little and we all carried matching pink umbrellas and the Danes were a friendly people who smiled on us.

On our honeymoon in Paris, Powell suddenly shouted from the hallway of the hotel. "Top! Top! Get out here quick. Help me carry Monique across the threshold."

Monique was enormously pregnant. On her honeymoon two roaring laughing men carried her across her threshold.

"Top, you two were drunk as skunks," Monique protested. "You couldn't even have carried Nita, and look how tiny she is."

"Nita," I said, "all I want to do is come home to you. That's what I'm living for—"

However much I had loved other wives and other women in between wives, I felt my heart and soul consumed by Nita. I could never get enough of her. I slept with her tight in my arms and in my thoughts and in my heart.

"It just shows how much you two love each other," Monique said.

We all have our dark sides, our night souls, and we are all prone to self-destruction.

*Always A Warrior* (Pocket Books, 1994)

My third time at marriage was not the charm. It was more like strike three. My first day home from the war, Nita said, "I've been having an affair." It was like she was trying to self-destruct.

She had seen him, slept with him, just a few nights before. I felt like a frag grenade with the pin pulled. Overcome with shock and grief and pain, I wanted to scream with rage, hurl myself against walls, jump in front of a truck.

"It didn't mean anything," Nita insisted. "It was just physical."

That was supposed to make me feel better?

I grabbed my pack and rode my bicycle furiously north in the July heat. I rode for days. Sometimes it rained, but mostly there was the burning sun, like in Saudi Arabia. I rode myself to exhaustion each day. One day across Oklahoma, Kansas and Missouri was like the day before and like the day after.

"Where are you going?" people sometimes asked.

"I'm a veteran," I said, as if that should explain everything.

"So, where are you going?"

"I don't know. I went to war. When I came home I found my new wife was sleeping around. Where would you go?"

I lost complete interest in writing for one of the few times in my life. Even while I was overseas, in the middle of war, I had continued writing. Now, I cared about nothing. All I thought about was that bicycle and the next sun-heated miles directly in front of me. I rode and rode until I literally fell from exhaustion near St. Louis.

I had had a wreck in a thunderstorm a day or so before and gashed open my knee. It was so swollen and infected I could hardly walk, much less peddle. I rented a motel room. There was stationery on the desk. I picked up a pen and I began to write again, letting out all the hurt and anger. I wrote the introduction and first chapter to *Always A Warrior*. And I kept writing.

That was a short marriage, the one interlude to my ten years of being single. Nothing remains once trust is violated.

### # # #

Success taught me that a single good book does not make a writer. Rather, success is the ability to repeat that process, to maintain inspiration and produce day in and day out. The task of writing does not become easier with each new project.

Writing is exhausting work. I have written and published as many as four books in a single year, along with a half-dozen magazine articles and miscellaneous other pieces. No one can keep up a pace like that day after day, year after year, without finding means to recharge his batteries. I have always turned toward wild places seeking rejuvenation.

When I was a kid, I would take off alone on foot into the Ozark Mountains and roam around for days at a time. Just I and two or three dogs. Hunting and fishing for our meals. When night came, I built a fire and sat by the blaze with the dogs and gazed into the coals, dreaming of those great adventures about which I would someday write. By the time I was thirteen or fourteen I was venturing as far as 100 miles from home.

It's a pattern I've continued every since. I call it going on "walkabout." I've hiked deserts and jungles and mountains all over the world—the tundra of Alaska, the elk plains of New Mexico, the Amazon, the Canadian forest, all the way across Guatemala... It's my method of recharging my writer's batteries. I come back refreshed and ready to go again.

> The Yukon Territory. Land of my boyhood heroes—Jack London and Sergeant Preston of the Royal Canadian Mounted Police. Just saying the name—*Yukon*—stirs up feelings of romance and adventure. The Klondike Gold Rush. Diamond Tooth Lil. Prospectors and fur trappers and explorers and Indians. Hudson Bay Company. A concentration of more inland grizzlies than anywhere else on the continent...
>
> Somewhere in that all but uncharted wilderness between the headwaters of the Big Salmon and Dawson City on the Yukon—a river distance of about 700 miles—I hoped to recognize my soul again.
>
> A canoe on a wild river offers an excellent platform from which to view the world. I found myself wanting the journey to go on and on, forever. It was a simple and primitive and satisfying existence. I lived for what the moment brought. Tomorrows do not exist in the wilderness. You eat, you sleep, you travel. You find yourself hoping you *never* reach your destination.
>
> "Canoeing In The Midnight Sun," *Action Digest*

One summer I lived on my 17-foot sailboat *Gandalf* in the anchorage at Key West, Florida. The cabin slept two. I kept an ice chest and a Coleman camp stove in the cockpit as a galley. I constructed a lap desk upon which I got in my daily writing.

Two separate classes of residents occupied the anchorage. Tied up next to shore were the magnificent houseboats, among which was one belonging to the singing rock-and-rollers *Bee-Gees*. The Conch Train stopped there every day to let tourists google and take pictures.

Out in the bay where I lived were the slums—ratty-looking houseboats, old cruisers whose engines had long ago been pawned, sails broken and twisted, rust and rot. Gulls and cormorants and pelicans perched on sunken boats whose prows stuck up out of the sea at low tide.

Sailing and living on my 17-foot sailboat *Gandalf* in the Caribbean.

My girlfriend, a six-foot stripper from *Pirate's Den*, lived on a tin houseboat. Her neighbors were a couple of lesbians, one of whom, built like a truck driver, often got drunk, picked fights with other sailors, and tossed them off the dingy dock into the water. On a run-down sloop lived an alcoholic female with cerebral palsy. She had to be lifted on and off boats. She developed a crush on me. Whenever she was drunk, which was most of the time, her voice rang out over the night water, "Chuck, will you come and sleep with me?" Laughter tinkled out of the other boats.

On a Kris Kraft long past seaworthiness lived a lonely young man who played the guitar and sang sad songs nearly every evening. We caught a large shark once and had a fish fry and party on a houseboat belonging to Bill Bailey and his girlfriend Jeannie. They both got drunk and got into a fight. Bill left paddling off into the darkness on a surfboard with his cat named Scavenger. Jeannie, swaying from too many beers, stood on the little back porch of her houseboat and began singing at the top of her lungs.

> *"Oh, won't you come home, Bill Bailey...?*
> *Oh, won't you come home...?*
> *I know I've done you wrong..."*

I loved to go out alone and sail the waters of the Florida Keys. I set off one morning for the Tortugas about 70 miles away. A trailing wind turned brisk by noon, and by afternoon I had squalls and six- to eight-foot seas. I reduced sails, relying on the jib, and had to tie myself into the cockpit to keep from being tossed overboard. It was a long and scary night before I finally came across a key, a small island, in the lee of which I double anchored to ride out the storm. Lighting flashed on the horizon and an eight-foot shark sliced the waters between my bow and anchor lines.

What writer, surrounded by characters and atmosphere like this, could resist being inspired? What a lucky man I was and am. Most beginning writers dream and pray for the opportunity to live such a life. It would never have happened, however, had I lost inspiration and given up in the early years.

In the Superstition Mountains of Arizona searching for the Lost Dutchman's gold.

# SECTION III:
# Goals

Aboard the nuclear aircraft carrier USS *Abraham Lincoln* from San Diego to Seattle.

89

# CHAPTER NINE

Setting goals for yourself is part of being a writer, without which you are wondering in the wilderness looking for bread crumbs. Inspiration takes care of itself if you set attainable goals and cultivate the discipline required for achieving them. Most people aim too low when they set goals. As a result, they do not give their best in order to expect life's best. The philosopher Santayana said you will at least catch a mountain if you reach for the moon. The lower you reach, the less you're likely to get.

It must have seemed to my family and those who knew me in the early years that I was indeed reaching for the moon when, at eight years old, I wrote my first novel, *Devil Mountain*. I kept telling everyone I was going to become a famous writer. In response, I was warned again and again that I was unlikely to ever reach such a goal. Famous writers were god-like figures who started out above the rest of us; they were *different*. How could a poor hill kid from Oklahoma ever expect to reach such heights?

Nevertheless, I said, I was going to do it.

"You have to have that feeling of 'I'll show them,'" said Leon Uris (*Exodus, Mila 18*). "If you don't have it, don't become a writer. It's part of the animal, but if you don't want to rise above the crowd, forget it."

I had the capacity as a kid, a trait I have retained throughout life, to isolate myself from circumstances unpleasant and escape into daydreams and fantasies about adventures and my future as a writer. That proclivity served me particularly well in those days when farmers grew cotton in the Arkansas River Valley from Webber Falls bottoms all the way through Arkansas and then down into the Deep South. We poor whites and poor blacks caught the "cotton truck," usually a two-ton truck with a tarp stretched over the bed, and were hauled out and cast into the endless fields before the sun came up.

It was back-breaking labor, bent over as the sun got hotter and beat down upon your neck and spine. The strap of the pick sack cut into your shoulders as you dragged it along the row, your hands nicked and bleeding and sore from plucking cotton out of bolls. You worked from light to dark and they paid you three bucks a hundred pounds. The most I ever picked was about a hundred a day; Mom sometimes got a few pounds more. Dad occasionally reached almost two hundred. My brother Joe picked less than I. Kenneth was never much of a hand, being the younger of us.

My body worked underneath the hot sun, but my mind was always somewhere else building castles in the air. I constructed this elaborate writer's life in which I was acclaimed a national treasure and my books became American classics. I would be awarded cars and a house of our own to live in and we would have ice cream every day. At the time, I still didn't realize you actually *sold* writing; I merely assumed rich people would pay me to write because I was a literary genius.

"What were you grinning about while you were picking?" Mom asked when we took lunch break and gathered around the weigh-in truck and the water barrel with its single community dipper. I must have been a strange kid.

"I was thinking about when I become a famous writer."

Tears came to her eyes and she hugged me and said nothing.

What I was doing subconsciously in those cotton fields was setting goals. They were becoming embedded in my psyche, rooted in my soul. Not only that, but I was also developing discipline and independence and self-reliance and other personal habits that would enable me to attain those goals, that would feed and nurture my dreams.

Several years ago I was asked to give the keynote address for the annual Junior Chamber of Commerce Awards Banquet in Wagoner, Oklahoma, a small city near my ranch. The Jaycees wanted me to talk about "success." I thought about it and I began by saying that it is much harder today for someone to come out of poverty and reach the moon than it was when I was a kid—not because there are more obstacles but instead because there are *fewer*. It is so much easier today for well-meaning people to steal your dreams.

At a castle in Germany.

Were I a kid living today as I lived then, in shacks and laboring in the fields at six years old, hordes of social workers would descend upon my family and assure us that, as a result of being "disadvantaged," we could do little for ourselves without the help of government. Food stamps and welfare would make us dependent, would rob us of our pride and eventually our souls. Why set goals when it is easier to lean back and survive on charity? Self-confidence greatly determines a person's success. How much self-confidence can you have when somebody else feeds you?

One year when times were exceptionally tough, Dad signed up for what he called "gimpy groceries." These were government surplus commodities for the poor—powdered milk and powdered eggs, cheese, canned meat, butter... Dad was too proud to go for them himself, so he sent me. I was about twelve years old. I wadded up a gunny sack in which to bring home the bounty and sneaked down back streets in Sallisaw to the city maintenance barn where the distribution took place.

I got in line with all the other poor people, so embarrassed that I kept trying to hide my face. I didn't move fast enough for one of the distribution workers. He came over and pushed me up in line.

"You can't do that!" I flared. I might have been only twelve years old, but other people still didn't push me around. Dad always said he'd beat me if I started a fight—but he'd also beat me if I refused to fight when I had to or if I lost a fight. In the hills, you fought to win, no matter what it took.

The maintenance worker got down in my face. "Boy," he snarled, "if the government feeds you, it'll do what it damned well pleases."

I have always remembered that. If somebody feeds you, he owns your soul. *Nobody* was going to own my soul. I had plans. I had goals. Didn't that goofy creature understand I was going to be a writer?

"Get in line."

"Touch me one more time and I'm gonna punch out your eyes."

Being in poverty doesn't scare me. I've been there before. What does scare me most is losing my liberty and independence to a Big Nanny government that promises to take care of us from cradle to grave—and which, in the process, robs us of our dreams. After I resigned from the police department to write full-time, I learned about something called an "earned income tax credit." Although I earned very little money and paid no income taxes at the moment, the government was *still* going to give me a "refund." Essentially, the government intended to give me someone else's money, a form of income redistribution.

I refused it, asking in a letter to the IRS why I should expect my neighbors to pay for choice I made. It wasn't up to my neighbors to take care of me. I would take care of myself. I had goals, I was a hard worker, I would succeed on my own.

Two neighbor farmers are raising sheep. Each raises on sheep a year, which is sufficient to fund his basic needs of food and shelter. Farmer Jones, however, is more ambitious and harder working than Farmer Smith.

Farmer Jones decides that he wants to give his family a better life. One year he decided to raise two sheep and use the income from the second sheep to add on to his house. He gets out of bed earlier, works later. Soon, his house is larger than Smith's.

Smith is satisfied to simply maintain his living standard on one sheep a year...

Time passes. Because of his initiative and drive, Farmer Jones prospers. Farmer Smith gets up one day, looks around. His fences are propped up, his house needs painting, and the transmission on his Farmall tractor has fallen out on the ground.

He looks over at Farmer Jones' place. By that time, Jones is raising three sheep a year. He has a new house, a new pickup truck with a camper, and he's out in his fields plowing every morning on a tractor so bright it shines in the sun.

"Why should I have so little," he asks himself, "when my neighbor has so much? It just ain't fair. I deserve more."

He has leaned the politics of greed and envy. He has learned he is a "victim."

The government agrees with him. It raises taxes on Farmer Jones. It takes one of Jones's sheep and gives it to his "disad-

vantaged" neighbor. After all, that is the fair and humane thing
to do...

Farmer Jones, wiping sweat from his brow, looks across
the fence at his laid-back neighbor resting in the shade. Farmer
Smith no longer raised any sheep. After all, why should he
work? The government is going to give him one of Jones's
sheep anyhow. He can live on one sheep and be satisfied.

Laid-back Farmer Smith lifts his head and grins at indus-
trious Farmer Jones. That angers Jones.

"I'll fix you, Smith!" he vows.

Next year, Farmer Jones cuts back on his work. Instead of
raising three sheep, he raises only two. After all, the government is going to seize the third sheep anyhow.

Farmer Jones has two sheep that year; Farmer Smith has
none. In the name of equality and compassion, the government
still takes one of Jones's two sheep and gives it to Smith.
Jones is right back where he started from. One sheep is just
enough to fund his basic needs of food and shelter...

"The Theory of Two Sheep," Tulsa *World*

This strong sense of independence was an integral part of my
makeup and figured prominently in all goals I set for myself as a
writer.

In the beginning days, I thought I was utterly alone in my
struggles to scribble words on paper. I thought I was unique in
that, while most writers were born, I was having to make myself
into one. As time went on, however, I learned that a great number of writers, perhaps the majority, had had to conquer
tremendous early hardships in order to achieve success—that
indeed there was no elevator to success. You had to take the
stairs.

James Michener began life as a foundling, a throw-away
baby taken in by a poor woman with a big heart. Mabel Michener gave James her name, since he had none of his own, and a
home. As it turned out, James was a restless youth with a wan-
derlust. He started hitchhiking around the country. He was going
to be a writer; he just didn't know how at the moment.

He worked a variety of odd jobs—spotter to catch short change artists at a carnival; a fortune teller named "Mitch the Witch;" a hotel night watchman; sportswriter... He traveled with a troupe of bullfighters in Spain, served as a chart boy on a Mediterranean coal boat, and joined a group collecting old ballads in the Hebrides. Eventually, after being arrested for vagrancy in Georgia, he attended Swarthmore College on a four-year scholarship.

World War II began and Michener wrote *Tales Of The South Pacific.* The rest, as the old saying goes, is history.

A surprisingly large number of writers possess similar credentials. John LeCarre described himself as a lonely boy whose father owned race horses and forced his family to live an "itinerate life." Stephen King's father, a sailor, abandoned his mother and him when Stephen was three years old. King worked a variety of early jobs as janitor, mill hand and laundry worker before he sold *Carrie.* Mary Higgins Clark was a middle-aged homemaker when her husband died, leaving her with no insurance, no income, and five children to feed and raise.

Why did these writers with difficult lives succeed when so many others failed? Because they possessed one other thing in common: They understood the reasoning and thinking behind the five magic steps to becoming a successful writer, and they applied them: discipline; inspiration; goal-setting; the use of ideas; and the development of craft. They knew what they wanted, they set goals, and they let nothing stop them.

Alex Haley (*Roots*) described how he worked toward his goal: "Ornately framed on my wall are two cans of sardines and 18 cents. In 1960, I was living in a one-room apartment in Greenwich Village. I was literally hanging on by my fingernails, trying to make it as a magazine writer. I was selling just enough to keep going from week to week, sometimes from day to day. In my little cupboard, I had these two cans of sardines that were all I had to eat in the world. And I had 18 cents in my pocket. That's not the same 18 cents by the way. I spent the original 18 cents on a cabbage for dinner that night. I remember thinking at the time, there's nowhere to go but up. And I put the two cans of sardines in a sack and put it away. Whenever I would move because I didn't have rent money, I would always take that sack with me. Six or seven years later I sold my first motion picture rights. That's when I had those two cans of sardines and that 18 cents framed. No matter where I go, it will always be displayed as a reminder of the most significant lesson in the world—that when you're pursuing a creative goal, you must hang in there. You must have faith. You must believe."

In 2001, my bio was included in *Who's Who In The World* and in *Who's Who In America* in 2002. I had dreamed such things in those cotton fields.

# CHAPTER TEN

Quotes are tacked and taped all over my office. One of my favorites is a simple three-liner: *I've always been called a dreamer, but never listened. I did what others dare not do. Lived my dream while they watched.* A second favorite is three words: *Eagles Don't Flock.* To follow dreams, to succeed at it, you have to be willing to break from the flock and, well, *go for it.*

The dreamer's greatest risk is in thinking too small. If your life is free of failure, it probably means you aren't reaching high enough and you aren't taking enough risks. I fell so many times while I was learning to walk as a writer that, figuratively, my hands and knees wore bruises on top of bruises. But I never lowered my goal, as do so many others when they suffer setbacks. My goal today remains the same as the mission statement I gave my mom when I was seven years old.

I want to live many lives—and write about it.

What is your mission statement, your declaration of what you ultimately intend to accomplish? Reach high. Just because you have your eye on the moon doesn't mean you have to grab it your first step out. In May 1961, U.S. astronaut Alan B. Shepard Jr.made America's first space flight—up and down for 15 minutes. John Glenn orbited the earth, three times, in 1962. Seven years later, on July 20, 1969, Neil Armstrong and Buzz Aldrin placed the first human footprints on the moon.

NASA's goal is to explore space, to go where no man has gone before. Shepard's 15-minute flight was one step toward that goal. Another step was rocketing men to the moon. Step by step. All goals are reached the same way.

You don't set out driving from Los Angeles and suddenly get to Chicago. You get there one leg at a time. You might not be able to see beyond your headlights, but you cover the ground anyhow while staying within the limits of your headlights. Be ambitious in your mission statement; be realistic in the intermediate legs. A budding novelist shouldn't attempt a task that would daunt a hardened vet. Herman Melville wasn't ready for *Moby Dick* until five novels into his career.

What do you *want*, how far do you want to go in your career as a writer? You must be brutally honest with yourself. I see three options, each of which builds upon the previous in order to reach the ultimate goal of freelance full-time writer/author. You can choose any of the three options as your goal, and that's fine. It's your personal decision. However, you shouldn't stop at a lower option unless that *is* your goal.

First of all, you can choose to simply write for your own pleasure, for self-expression. Perhaps keep a journal, record a family history, express yourself without thought of commercial publication.

All writers go through this first option. I began writing because it provided me great pleasure to do so. It gave meaning to my young life, it opened up a new world of hope in which my imagination carried me past three-room shacks and cotton fields.

On Saturdays when we went to town in the wagon pulled by the red one-eyed mule and the big black mare, and later in an old pickup truck, my brothers and I could go to the movies for ten cents each. We watched Rex Allen, Roy Rogers, Gene Autry. A second feature starred The Three Stooges or the Bowery Boys. That was followed by a cartoon, Coming Attractions, a news reel, and a serial thriller that always ended with a hero going over a cliff of having a train wreck or getting shot. *Will he live or die? Come back next week to see the next thrilling episode...*

I loved movies with real heroes; I loved stories with heroes. I wrote most of the day on Sunday after seeing movies on Saturday, re-telling the movie story. "Jody the boy came running over the hill with his dog, Old Yeller..." I re-wrote *The Yearling* from the movie, *The Horse And The Lion*, and any number of westerns and Tarzans.

I did the same thing with books. I copied Hemingway's *For Whom The Bell Tolls* from cover to cover, like a medieval monk bent over a parchment of the Bible laboring to make his own copy. I re-wrote *Grapes Of Wrath* and *Gulliver's Travels*. Although I didn't realize it at the time, I was learning and practicing the craft of writing, doing it because it thrilled me to put words on paper, even somebody else's words, and see the story come alive inside my imagination.

Winter warfare training with U.S. Army Special Forces.

There were only two or three boys in my high school typing class. The rest of the students were girls, since typing was considered "sissy," like home economics. I was very handy with my fists, however, which prevented a lot of peer ragging. I learned to type 120 words per minute, burning up those old manual Underwoods and Royals. The first time I typed one of my manuscripts, I carried it around for days reading it and looking at it. It was in *print*, almost like a real book.

There was nothing modest about my goal. However, the steps toward achieving that goal slowly evolved. I wrote first because it pleased me. I learned how to type my manuscripts and longed for the day when I possessed my own wonderful typewriter—an opportunity which came only after I enlisted in the navy and got rich earning $56 a month. Winning the $25 in the writing contest when I was 15 launched me immediately into considering a second option. For some, perhaps, the first option is enough. Not for me.

### # # #

The second-option writer publishes a piece now and then, but is content, at least initially, to write part-time while otherwise holding down a steady day job. There are literally thousands of them in the United States. They write for local newspapers, submit stories to the literary "little" magazines, and thrill over seeing their bylines in trade, technical or professional journals. I call them the amateur writers who make up the farm teams from whose ranks eventually emerge professional freelancers. I served my time on the farm teams.

> Flood's breathing came nasal in the basement beneath the ring. That was because of the scar tissue. The basement smelled of sweat and blood and piss and old socks. It was a familiar odor to flood, old locker rooms were, although he couldn't smell much anymore because of his nose.
>
> Arn wrapped his hands for him while Flood sat regarding the up-and-comer shadow boxing at the other end of the locker room.
>
> "We can still call the fight," Arn said.
>
> Flood wasn't listening. He was remembering the year he topped the heavyweight card at Las Vegas's Caesar's Palace.
>
> "Yes," Flood said absently.
>
> "Yeh? What the hell does that mean?"
>
> "It means *yeh*, Arn. Uh, that's what it means."
>
> There was a knockdown upstairs. The fight crowd cheered. The fight crowd was small. Down the street, a speech by the local precinct captain drew a bigger crowd...
>
> "The Up-And-Comer," *The DeKalb Literary Arts Journal*

Did I mention that I was a fighter on a navy boxing team? You are quite astute if you detected a flavor of Hemingway in the above short story. I was still in my formative years, about nineteen, and trying to develop my voice.

I enlisted in the navy intent on becoming a journalist—an intermediate step on my way to the moon. I figured to attend JO (journalist) school to learn about writing and then polish my skills as a newspaper reporter. The recruiter promised I had a chance if my test scores were high enough. He couldn't promise anything though. Journalists in the navy were relatively rare.

Although my test scores were high, the navy decided it needed yeomen more than it needed journalists. A yeoman is a clerk. Photographs of me in the boot camp class book receiving my orders show an 18-year-old kid whose face drags the ground from disappointment. I ended up as a chaplain's yeoman at Naval Air Station, Whidbey Island, Washington, but soon transferred to Operations.

Disappointment out of Navy boot camp when I receive my orders (center). I had wanted to go to journalism school.

I had my own goals. I would not be thwarted.

In Operations, I volunteered to start, write and publish an aviation safety bulletin called *Whidbey Approach*. It was still in production when I was discharged on April Fool's Day 1964. Then I paid a visit to the editor of the base newspaper *Prop Wash*, and begged him to give me a chance. I promised to work for him full-time on evenings and weekends while also holding down my yeoman's job at Ops.

For over six months, I pulled my full weight in both positions. I was ambitious and creative. Soon, I was turning in feature copy that had commanders and other personnel on base calling *Prop Wash* asking for me personally to do their stories. These were my first attempts at "participatory journalism."

> We were alone now, each man for himself. We had parachuted into enemy territory, survived for a week, and now must pass through enemy lines to safety.
>
> Carefully, using the terrain to the best advantage. I circled across two hills. Barely ten minutes from the beginning, rifle fire clattered both to my left and right, and machine gun fire ahead. But I saw no one. For 30 minutes I hid in a nettle patch. I heard men passing to either side. Gunfire stuttered. More students caught...
>
> I traveled, studied and dashed across roads, and all the while after that first hour gunfire was in the distance. Only once did I spot the enemy. A lone rifleman crossed within 20 feet of where I hid without spying me...
>
> "Survival Training—How To Live After You're Gone,"
> *Prop Wash*

I was appointed *Prop Wash* feature editor when the next opening occurred. I moved form Ops to the newspaper office, whistling and singing all the way. I was moving on up. Learning how to set goals and reach them. One night I stood outside and looked up at the moon and said, "Watch out, moon. I'm coming."

Option two is like a training camp where you prepare yourself to assault Mount Everest on your way to the moon. This is where you learn your trade, your craft, and develop essential character traits of discipline, independence, and perseverance that will allow you to make the break. I must have written at least three million words from 1962 when I went on *Prop Wash* until I quit my job as a copy in 1979 to move into the tool shed and commit myself to writing. Most of that vast production was never published, was in fact, looking at it in retrospect, unpublishable. Bad as it might have been, however, it didn't mean I was failing. I was actually succeeding. You fail only if you stop writing.

"Most beginners think that writing is a quick ticket to some kind of celebrity status, to broads and talk shows," John D. MacDonald observed. "Those with that shallow motivation can forget it... If he or she is not willing to commit one million words to paper—ten medium long novels—without much hope of ever selling one word, in the process of learning this trade, then forget it. And if he or she can be discouraged by anyone in this world from continuing to write, write write—then forget it."

# # #

I spent seventeen years in the second option before I moved into the third—full-time freelance writer. It is estimated that there are less than 5,000 full-time freelancers actually making a living at it in the United States. Don't be daunted by statistics. Unlike baseball farm teams in which players must wait for someone else to select them for the majors, the writer uses his own judgment. We appoint ourselves to the major league. *We* prepare and then *we* choose to move on up in pursuit of our goals.

# CHAPTER ELEVEN

Goals are like New Year's resolutions—useless unless you commit to them. Commitment means an investment of your soul and your heart as well as your intellect.

"I more or less gave up everything else in my life," said former Secret Service agent Gerald Petievich (*Shakedown, Earth Angels*). "I went to bed early every night. I had no social life. On the job I refused promotions just so I could stay in one place and write. That's the line of commitment you have to make for fiction. But when you take on that kind of obsession—which is what writing is, what art is—nothing else can stop you if you choose to do it."

I agree with his idea of commitment. Writing is not merely something you *do*; it is what you *are*. Life and writing are not two separate entities. However, you don't have to give up your life to be a writer. In the committed writer, they meld into a single whole.

In 1997, I went to Spain and ran with the bulls in the annual *feria*, as Hemingway had done. In 1999, I backpacked and camped across Egypt and the Sudan with my wife Donna Sue, riding camels into the desert and camping out. In between, I climbed Mt. Rainier in Washington because I had never climbed a mountain before and I wanted the experience. In 2000, I helped a friend, Alaskan big game guide Les Cobb, ride, lead and drove a ramuda of horses 150 miles across the Alaskan wilderness, crossing the Yukon River by log raft, in order to have the horses available for hunters at a moose hunting camp. In 2001, I set world records by being the first to pilot a Powered Parachute ultralite aircraft from coast to coast...

See what I mean? I write to live and I live to write. It's a symbiotic relationship. One is inconceivable without the other. Naturally, my experiences end up in books or articles sooner or later. For example, my hero in *Detachment Delta: Operation*

*Punitive Strike* (Avon, 2002) escapes from Afghanistan in a Powered Parachute.

At the bull ring in Pamplona, Spain, following the Running of The Bulls.

In my commitment to the art and craft of writing, I thought in the beginning that you had to be formally educated in order to be a writer. I took courses in "creative writing" wherever I happened to be—at Skagit Valley Junior College in Washington, at

Tulsa Junior College in Oklahoma, at Miami-Dade Junior College in Florida. I grew more and more disillusioned and skeptical with each course I took.

By the time I made it to Florida State University, I had all but given up on the idea that writing can be taught, at least taught in the manner I experienced it. I majored in History and Anthropology, because they were subjects that interested me, and minored in Sociology and American Literature for the same reason. I took one writing course at FSU. The course concentrated on "literature." On symbols and metaphors, on "what the author *really* meant," and about how, as the professor put it, "You should never compromise your artistic integrity. You may never be widely read, but that is the cross we must bear in order to be an important writer of prose."

In other words, don't concern yourself with the *hoi polloi,* the common unwashed, and with earning a living as a writer. According to such a narrow interpretation, if a book sells well and is popular it automatically means it isn't literature. All those people out there reading Mary Higgins Clark and Tony Hillerman haven't the refined tastes of their intellectual betters in academia, and the writers are compromising their "artistic integrity" in writing for them.

I was eking out a C in class, primarily because I wouldn't be shaken from my stubborn premise that story telling is the art of the ordinary people for the ordinary people, not some intellectual exercise. Homer and Shakespeare knew that. Finally, in disgust, I clipped together a thick file of my published articles and short stories and turned them in with a note across the front: *Kiss my ass.*

I got an A in the course.

I have taken no other writing courses since then, although I teach them now. I teach practical writing the way I learned it—story telling for real people, not eggheads.

Condescension and antipathy toward "popular" writers prevail throughout the so-called "literary world." I long ago accepted that it is unlikely I shall receive any major writing awards, even from my home state, because I write so often outside and even against the prevailing orthodoxy of what constitutes "literature," or what is "socially acceptable" or "politically correct" in intellectual circles. I write gritty, down-in-the-streets stuff about cops and wars, rough men and women who don't know which fork to use first and will tell you to kiss off in a heartbeat.

I've published 40 or so books and novels in both hardcover and paperback, many of them histories of important people, but they are histories written for the popular and not the academic market. So who gets all the awards and are inducted into State Writers Halls of Fame? A black man who writes *two* books about the experience of growing up black; a second-rate radical feminist poet; a woman who published one out-of-print literary novel years ago...

Understand, I begrudge none of them. I simply note the antipathy toward popular writers and the prevailing prejudice against writers who fall outside the narrow realm of what is considered literature. I'm not the only one to remark on it.

R.V. Cassill, who retired as professor of English at Brown University, shocked his audience by a speech he delivered at the Associated Writing Programs' anniversary in Boston. Cassill had himself formed the AWP because he believed that "the teaching of writing should be a part of literary education" and that a degree in writing "would give writers a certain status, as the PhD did for scholars.' He now changed his mind.

He recommended that in today's politically correct climate the writer should get out of academia, arguing that political compromises a writer must make regarding university politics and ideological compromises such as political correctness are anathema to the creative writer.

"University politics have gone on forever," Cassill said, "but never so dangerous as it has become; and particularly for the writer who takes it upon himself to be the conscience of his race, if your conscience has been compromised then the whole fictive audience whom you wish to address is poisoned too."

"I don't think a college degree is necessary to become a good writer," Edward Abbey wrote. "I'm not even certain it's an advantage. College probably won't *hurt* you—if you don't take it too seriously."

"Life is terrible and is lived in the streets and in the fields, and the place for the writer-to-be, therefore, is in the fields and in the streets..." Nelson Algren insisted. "I think it's wrong to believe that literature begins at the top with the most articulate and that our best writers should be the most educated and should write of the people who are most articulate and most socially important. It's always unpleasant to think that there's more vitality in the gutters than in the penthouses, and yet it's true..."

A writer's commitment should be to his craft, to his writing, not to the vagaries of the chatter around him. If your goal is to be a "literary" writer, go for it—but keep your day job. Set your goals and commit because that is what you want to do, not because it is expected and seems superior to writing westerns or suspenses or romances. On the other hand, if you want to make a living as a writer, your best shot is to concentrate upon writing for real people out there who actually buy books and read them.

The contrast between the two philosophies of writing is best exemplified in the magazines *Writer's Digest* and *Poets & Writers Magazine. Writer's Digest*, for which I have written, is the best on the market for both the new and established writer. I discovered it when I was about seventeen years old and have subscribed to it regularly ever since. It's a nuts and bolts publication devoted to writers who want to compete in the open market and *sell* what they write. It is unpretentious, wholeheartedly *laissaiz faire*, and directed toward the working writer in the popular mass field.

One look at *Poets & Writers Magazine* underscores the difference in the level of goals and commitments of its readership. *Writer's Digest* preaches *market. Poets & Writers* concentrates upon the "literary" and has a pretentious and condescending tone to it. Not surprisingly, since the magazine is partly government-funded, it often instructs its refined readers in the methods for obtaining grants and public funds. Commit yourself, certainly, but learn to depend upon other people's money to help you reach your goal.

A professor I knew at Northeastern State University in Oklahoma received a $30,000 grant from the government-funded National Endowment for The Arts (NEA) to write a novel, the publication of which was uncertain. At the same time, I received a $10,000 advance on royalties for a Pocket Books novel, the publication of which was assured. It irked me then and irks me now that I competed to *earn* my advance while he sought a government handout. Some of the taxes I paid on my advance were granted by the NEA to the professor so he could take time off from work to write his novel. I competed on the open market, he sucked from it. This incident and others like it led to a spirited exchange in several issues of *Poets & Writers* between myself and some of the readers.

I agree completely with R.T. Smith about the role of art and artists in our society. Indeed, art supplies that arena in which a culture examines its values and preserves that which is beautiful and meaningful.

I disagree, however, and disagree vehemently with the implied suggestion that writers and other artists somehow *deserve* public funding. Inherent in such thought is the assumption that the common masses do not appreciate "real art" enough to pay for it on their own. Only the elite, the cultured, the refined value it. Therefore, the public must be taxed to support "real art," whether it wants it or not. Pay for it and shut up. It's for your greater moral good.

Conversely, such thought assumes that any art that commoners like and appreciate enough to voluntarily support cannot be "real art." Everyone knows the masses have their taste buds in their jeans. A writer or painter who becomes commercially successful, who makes a living at his art or craft, is automatically suspect. The "real artist" with important things to express for the greater good of mankind suffers for his art—and demands tax money to support himself while he writes the Great American Novel or dunks crucifixes in urine.

There is something patently offensive in the smugness with which recipients demand welfare from the NEA, as though endowment are their due by virtue of their superior creative contributions. R.T. Smith preened about how the grant he received "allowed me to travel and to concentrate on improving my craft." Another acquaintance of mine received a $30,000 grant that allowed him to take off one year to write a novel. He had published nothing significant before—and the novel he wrote on the grant has never been published.

I and other commercial artists pay for our own travel. We improve our craft by working at it on our own without demanding our neighbors' tax money to provide our "creative juices," as one NEA grant recipient put it, "the freedom from the daily grind." We professionals must produce or we don't get paid. We don't expect welfare. The taxes we pay in pursuing our art then go toward helping to support those whose art won't support them.

I do understand the difficulty in breaking into the arts and earning a living in the creative field. For many years I worked "regular" jobs while I got up every morning at 4:00 a.m. to write. Still, in spite of the hardships, we make our own career choices. It is the height of arrogance to then insist on public support for our choices simply because the apprenticeship is tough and we are creative people. Why should the public be forced to pay for an artist's contribution any more than it should be compelled to grant a plumber or an electrician the opportunity "to travel and to concentrate on improving my craft?"

I believe the public commercial process preserves that which is meaningful in our culture. After all, Pat Conroy and John Irving are doing quite well. *The Phantom of The Opera* is a world-wide commercial success. For that matter, I'm doing fine. For would-be artists and prima donnas to howl for public charity because they can't make it on their own is an insult to those who have struggled through apprenticeships to their own successes.

It is a subtle form of tyranny for any government, for whatever high or noble cause, to seize my money to pay for something I may not want. If a writer pens a good book, it will sell on its own merit. If a ballerina is good enough, an actor powerful enough, a painter inspired enough, each will find a public receptive to his talents.

Let R.T. Smith pay for his own travels. Don't make me pay for them. I'll pay for my own...

"Letters," Poets & Writers Magazine

Take a look at *Amazon.com*. Think you'll find "R.T. Smith" on it with any of the books he's published? To my way of looking at it, nothing is more detrimental to the budding writer than to accept—even *demand*—preferential treatment because he's an "artist." All he's doing is taking "gimpy groceries" and selling his commitment. If you're going to write, set that as a goal and make the commitment. Don't expect me or other taxpayers to take up the slack because you can't cut it. You either make it or you don't. Few, if any, successful writers depended upon "gimpy groceries" to make it to the top.

Setting a goal and making a commitment to achieving it is both difficult and a tremendous risk. It can be very scary. However, it can be even more scary *not* reaching for your dream. How many people have you heard complaining about things they *could* have done, *should* have done, or *wished* they had done in order to realize a dream? They felt defeated because they had never even *tried.*

One of the quotes above my desk, attributed to various great men, celebrates those why try against the odds:

"The credit belongs to the man who is actually in the arena, whose face is marred by dust and sweat and blood; who, at the best, knows in the end the triumphs of high achievement and who, at the worst, if he fails, at least fails while daring greatly, so that his place shall never be with those cold and timid souls who know neither victory nor defeat."

# CHAPTER TWELVE

You have set your goal high, you've prepared yourself with discipline, inspiration, ideas and craft to support your goal, and now you're ready to do it—make the break to option three and become a full-time freelance writer. You are ready to become one of what Harlan Ellison called "the poor, damned souls who must write, who haven't any more choice in the matter than whether or not they breathe."

Don't get hasty. It might not be the best idea to get miffed at work one day and quit your job on the thought that you'll sell something next month to keep the paychecks coming in. You will need to prepare yourself further before you move into your own tool shed. It was nearly two years from the time I advised my wife Dianne that I wanted to write full-time—and she promptly divorced me—until I actually made the break. During those two years, I prepared to *begin* my new full-time career.

In making these preparations, there are several factors you must take into consideration. Family, if you are married, should be the first of these. Quite obviously, I had little family support. To begin with, Dianne and I simply had different philosophies on life. She treasured security and routine, comfort without surprises. I was a risk taker.

I pilot small aircraft and when David was a year-and-a-half old I took him for his first flight in a rented Cessna. The wonder that beamed in his small face as he viewed the earth and the clouds from the sky remains one of my most cherished memories. He took to flying like a bird, was frightened the first time in a boat, but fast became boldly fond of motorcycles. When I take him riding in his large helmet he sits snuggled safely between my knees, holding tightly to the gas cap...

"Enrich Your Baby's World," *Parents' Your New Baby*

If your spouse is opposed to the idea of a risky career change, either the spouse or the career will eventually have to go. Dianne had little faith that I could and would provide; she was unwilling to face any rock challenges that might come along. Part of the reason she bailed out was because of the obvious lack of security that confronted us while I made my new start. She wasn't having any of my argument that everything in life is uncertain.

Kathy abandoned ship, I think, primarily because of the stress involved in my being a combat correspondent. "I'm not going to be here when they bring your body home," she said. And—*Poof!*

As for Nita, I don't consider her a *real* wife, the marriage ended so quickly. She was the only one who wasn't a direct casualty of my writing, although indirectly my personality of wandering off to go to wars might have contributed to her own wandering. For her, parting while I was away in *Desert Storm* did not lead to her heart growing fonder.

Some five years or so after Nita, when I was about 53-years-old, I met the perfect woman to become a writer's wife. Donna Sue and I met at a Christmas party. She was 49, blond, petite, pretty, outgoing, and an independent, successful businesswoman. With the biggest heart. Absolutely the best human being I had come across in a lifetime of banging around the world.

At the party was a huge balloon that, when busted, showered favors, among which were free tickets to the Caribbean. I had been dancing with Donna Sue when the time came for balloon breaking. "I'm always lucky," I assured her. "I've been stabbed, shot once, and I'm still alive."

"I'm not lucky," she said. "I've been married twice and both husbands died."

The first drowned, the second succumbed to cancer.

"I have enough luck for both of us," I said.

I did indeed. We didn't win the free trip to the Caribbean, but we were married a year later. One of the first places I took her was fly fishing to New Mexico. I knew I had a keeper when she waded right into the stream among the bulrushes. She learned to snow ski that same year and to sail a boat. She accompanied me backpacking to Egypt and was nearly mugged in Spain while I was running with the bulls. She opted out of going with me to the Amazon to study flora and fauna for a new Tulsa Zoo rainforest exhibit. She's gone halibut and salmon fishing in Alaska, but draws the line at roaming the tundra hunting caribou.

"People get married and the first thing they want to do is change each other," she philosophized. "I'd never try to stop him from going anywhere he wants to go or doing anything he needs to do."

And she hasn't. It's part of her own independence and self-sufficiency, her strength.

Training a colt on my Oklahoma horse ranch.

At our horse ranch I always have a bunch of colts and young horses to train for roping and cowboying. I'm developing an equilibrium problem as I grow older. One afternoon, I trailered a young horse-in-training to a roping competition in Coweta. At home in our own arena, Smoky and I were busting steers one after the other. We were salty.

"Smoky and I are going to win some money," I told Donna Sue.

About 200 cowboys showed up for Bill Lanterman's roping. Smoky wasn't accustomed to crowds and excitement; the poor pony shattered under the pressure. He was young and incredibly quick. I had trained him to trail by chasing peacocks. Not only did I fall off my horse, I fell of *twice*. I had been a professional rodeo bronc rider on weekends in Washington, Oregon and Idaho in the 1960s while I was still in the navy. I just didn't fall off horses like that. I came limping home.

"Don't you think it's about time you gave up a few things?" Donna Sue asked. I was 60-years-old.

"I haven't lived all my lives yet," I responded.

"It's all a part of him," Donna Sue said when the sons and grandkids expressed concern. "Why should I try to stop him from living? I could no more do it anyhow than I could stop him from writing."

She's the kind of spouse you want. I'm certain had I had her at the beginning I wouldn't have been married so many times.

Let us assume then that you are either single or that you have a spouse like Donna Sue willing to support your decision to begin freelancing. The next factor you need to consider is your publishing credits, your body of work.

If you aren't already publishing regularly, making money at it, don't even think of quitting your day job yet. You'll likely starve out, get discouraged, lose sight of your goal, and quit in despair. Ninety five percent of all writers who begin freelancing give up before the first year is over—primarily because they fail to prepare. The other five percent reach varying levels of success, often taking employment as editors or newspaper reporters.

My first novel was already accepted for publication before I resigned from the Tulsa police department. I was also marketing two or three articles a month to the detective magazines and was well-established as a crime writer. Kathy, Joshua and I might not live like Vanderbilts when we moved into the tool shed, but we weren't going to starve. I was earning money writing *before* I quit my job. That was important; that was vital.

You aren't going to live well at the beginning anyhow, unless you were born with the proverbial silver spoon in your mouth or your spouse is willing to support you—in which event you're dependent on someone else and not really making your way at writing. Alex Haley lived in a ratty Greenwich Village rented room in the early days when he began freelancing, as did Norman Mailer and Arthur Miller. That brings us to a third factor for consideration: overhead for necessities such as rent and food. Even if you think cheap, inexpensive, basics, you're still going to need a buffer to carry you through for a year or so.

I recommend that you have sufficient savings to last at least a year even if you sell nothing. An emergency rainy day fund. Savings may rapidly become depleted by a crisis, such as when wild dogs attacked Joshua. It helps also if you have some form of supplemental income. I stayed in the Army Reserves, which afforded me at least a regular, thought small, paycheck. Some writers continue to work part time.

Prior to changing careers, I bought a plot of land and saved money for a year in advance. My family and I lived in the tool shed rent-free while I built our *real* house in stages I could afford. Virtually our only expenses that first year were food and medicine, gas for the pickup truck, and utilities once we obtained water and electricity. I owned the five acres, so we weren't going to get kicked off for back payments or not paying rent. There was no mortgage on the real house when I completed it. The old pickup was lien-free, and I had few other liabilities.

Fortunately, each time we faced the wolf at our closet door, I'd sell another story or article to keep our dreams fueled...

What counted was that we had succeeded in building a farm pioneer style, my writing was selling well, and we looked forward to a future far brighter than the more confined one we had left in the city...

The house is all but completed now, a pretty little cabin of native stone. Behind it sets the tool shed.

Sometimes we look at it and, for all the hardships we endured, we miss our "homesteading" days.

For it was there, in that tool shed, that we learned the satisfaction of honest labor for one's own comfort, the pleasures of a free sunset, a basic lifestyle, and the independence of awaking each day and knowing that that day, for better or worse, belongs to you...

"Homesteading In A Tool Shed," *Oklahoma Rural News*

No matter how much you prepare, however, there will never be a perfect time to make the move. You do everything you can in advance—set your goal; learn and work at your craft; arrange necessities such as a place to live, emergency and rainy day funds and the support of your family; consider all conditions and contingencies—and, then, one day, simply bite the bullet and go for it. Wait for the perfect time in life to do anything and you'll never do it.

In 1997 I climbed Mount Rainier. Seventeen members of the climbing team started the assault. Seven of us summated; I was one of the seven. The others dropped off one by one along the way due to fatigue, altitude sickness, or simply because they hadn't the fortitude to continue stomping one crampon boot in front of the other.

Wind blew at 50mph that high up. The temperature was 30 below and the air was so thin that my lungs rasped in my chest. I was so weak I could hardly stand. My cheeks were frost-nipped and ice weighed heavy in my brows, lashes and mustache. I felt like vomiting from altitude sickness.

Nonetheless, I stood on the snowy point of the peak, the tallest in the continental United States, and looked out over that vast beautiful world. I was filled with exhilaration. I was on top of the world! Through my own resources and guts and strength and will

I had conquered this mountain. I would not have given up that moment for all the riches in the world.

It was precisely the same feeling I get every time I publish a book and know that I have what it takes to reach the goal I set for myself so long ago.

On the summit of Mt. Rainier in Washington.

# SECTION IV:
# Ideas

*"Every person you meet—and everything you do in life—is an opportunity to learn something. That's important to all of us, but most of all to a writer because as a writer you can use anything."*

— *Tom Clancy*

On the Amazon River in Peru.

# CHAPTER THIRTEEN

"Doesn't the well *ever* run dry?"

The question of where I get my ideas and how I develop them is invariably asked whenever I speak or teach about writing. Don't I ever find myself coming up dry on new ideas for novels, nonfiction books, or magazine articles? The answer is *never*. I might if I merely waited for ideas to fall like rain from the sky to fill my well. However, the best wells don't depend solely upon rainfall. You have to dig your well deep enough to tap into those vast networks of underground springs and streams so that when you draw out one idea, another flows in.

While ideas spring from hundreds of sources, curiosity is the cornerstone, the mother lode of ideas without which no writer can hope to keep his well from running dry. Curiosity about life and its substance has led me into far-flung corners of the world and into personal experiences that provide ideas while they flavor my finished product with a reality, an authenticity, that can only be achieved by being there. Seeing for myself, doing. Inquiring minds want to know. I've been bitten by a piranha in the Amazon (his jaws are now in my library), stranded on an island in Canada with a grizzly, trampled by a bucking horse in an Oregon rodeo, dived for Sir Francis Drake's treasure off Costa Rica, crashed airplanes in Washington and Oklahoma...

The old bronzeback crashed the surface of the coffee-colored Suwannee, a gill-rattling, tail-walking lunker big enough to easily snap my two-pound line. But a big bass with two-pound line and 25 yards of river separating us was no challenge at all compared to that of initiating a tenderfoot wife into the wonders of the Great Outdoors. At the same time I hooked the fish, my wife, 5-year-old son, and half-grown puppy spotted a seven-foot alligator gliding across the bow of the canoe. Pandemonium set in, with a general outcry about how we were all going to be devoured alive while I stubbornly hung onto a dumb fish...

"Initiation On the Suwannee," *Fur-Fish-Game*

Curiosity and the ideas curiosity generate begin with what the newspaper business calls the "five W's and the H." *Who, what, when, where, why* and *how.* Take the example of the so-called "homeless." Ever since the conscience-raising days of the 1960s, the subject of the homeless surfaces during every national election in order for politicians to demonstrate their compassion and concern. Newspapers and news magazines blare accusatory headlines of neglect and social failure in our treatment of the homeless. While I read prodigiously, of course, I seldom take everything I read as the final word on any subject. Curiosity about the homeless—who they were, what they did, where they were, how they lived, and why they were in such dire straits—compelled me to go out and find the answers for myself.

Depending upon who you believe, there are from 250,000 to 3 million "homeless" people blighting up the citysides in the United States—"abandoned Americans" starving in doorways and freezing when the winter storms blow...

I became one of the homeless to learn about them. Wearing ragged jeans and my old leather go-to-hell cap that had seen me through such as the war in El Salvador. I grabbed a handful of the first freight train that came along and "rode the rails" across mid-America, living on skid rows and American backstreets from Oklahoma to Michigan—Tulsa, Kansas City, St. Louis, Chicago and, finally, Detroit.

The first freight I caught, I simply reached out and grabbed it as it passed. It almost jerked me out of my socks. There is a trick to catching a moving freight.

There is a trick to getting off one too. You get off before the train enters the railyards and the railroad bulls catch you.

One thing I found out quickly. In spite of all the hyperbole about the hungry in America, no one is starving to death. In two weeks, I actually gained weight on a high starch diet of macaroni and cheese, potato and fat meat stews, bread and donuts, with lots of sugar in tea or black coffee. The fare on the streets was plain and cheap, but it was free and there was always plenty of it...

"Living Among Homeless," *OKmagazine*

"The best work that I've ever done always has a feeling of having been excavated," Stephen King observed. "I don't feel like a novelist or a creative writer as much as I feel like an archaeologist who is digging things up and brushing them off and looking at the carvings on them. Sometimes you get a little pot out of the ground, and that's a short story. Sometimes you get a bigger pot, which is a novelette. Sometimes you get a building, which is like a novel."

I like the imagery of excavating from life and using it in my writing. An archaeologist of human experiences.

One afternoon in El Salvador while I was in-country covering the civil war, I hopped one of those wonderful psychedelic-painted buses from San Salvador out to Las Palmas. There were about 20 people hanging onto the luggage rack on top since the inside was already crammed, a plastic Jesus on a dashboard festooned with beads, a turkey with its feet tied lying in the aisle, and, toward the back, an old woman carrying a piglet in a canvas bag in her lap.

A gorgeous young woman got on at one of the war-zone villages. Beautiful honey-brown face with enormous dark sad eyes you could melt into. But it wasn't her face and eyes that attracted me as much as it was her peasant garb and her hands. Her hands were as large as mine. Brown and strong and sinewy. Capable-looking hands, work-hardened and calloused.

My curiosity went wild. Who was she? What was she doing here? How did she live? Who and where were her husband and children? Were they fighting the war? Was *she* involved in the war?

I filed that image away and let my imagination work on it. A few years later I went to Mexico with a group of oceanographers from the University of Mexico to study sea lion diet and its impact on fisheries. We SCUBA-dived with sea lions off Cedros Island and camped out on the desert with pink rattlesnakes. Such is the way curiosity spurs creative thought that the girl from the bus in El Salvador became Luz in the fishing village on Cedros.

> The *mujeres* whispered over whose baby it might be. The younger women giggled and averted their eyes. The men of the village had never spoken to Luz anyhow except in the night when they came to her room, and they had never spoken much then. Even the *alcalde*, the mayor, favored close scrutiny of the cove by the cannery whenever Luz came laboring along the village streets in the dust...
> "Luz," *Amelia*

My imagination has used this woman in one form or another in a number of works of fiction and will probably continue to use her. It's a part of Stephen King's "excavating" from life, capturing in the mind those vivid images that later become part of your work.

"When you walk into a room and get a certain feeling or emotion," Ernest Hemingway counseled, "remember back until you see exactly what it was that gave you the emotion. Remember what the noises and smells were and what was said. Then write it down, making it clear so that the reader will see it, too, and have the same feeling you had."

> The drive entailed moving twelve horses from Cobb's Lost Creek Ranch near Eureka to a fall moose hunting camp along the Yukon River downstream of the Indian village, Tanana. That meant riding, leading, and driving the ramuda across a mountain range to the river, crossing the Yukon, then following it downstream through swamps and across feeder creeks to the moose camp, a journey of approximately 150 miles...
> Cold autumn rains, a prelude to the approaching Alaskan winter, fell every day in the high country. Steady downfalls that soaked leather, clothing, hair, skin, and morale. Every-

thing mildewed. Wet camps were made with a tarp stretched for shelter and fires blazing in futile attempts to dry clothing and equipment. Weary wranglers too exhausted to care crawled into damp bedrolls...

"Banker Turns Alaskan Wrangler," *Alive*

Curiosity about people, places, things, events, about life, leads to involvement, which leads to ideas. Curiosity about the Spanish Civil War inspired Ernest Hemingway to go, to see, and to write *For Whom The Bell Tolls*. James Jones's service as a peacetime soldier in Hawaii resulted in *From Here To Eternity*. Harper Lee's personal experiences as a child in a small southern town led to *To Kill A Mocking Bird*. Charles Dickens fictionalized a version of his boyhood in *David Copperfield*.

Flying a powered parachute. I made the first transcontinental flight in the ultralite aircraft.

I'm neither recommending nor even suggesting that you must be an adventurer and constantly defy danger in order to cultivate ideas and become a successful writer. Far from it. I'm merely showing you how I do it to achieve my stated goal of "living many lives and writing about them." However, I am saying that whether your life consists of parachuting out of airplanes over Africa or of taking long walks through the zoo on weekends, it is your curiosity and awareness of life around you, not where you are or what you're doing, that spurs the imagination and leads to those personal experiences that define the successful professional writer. You can "excavate" in your own home town.

During the mid to late 1980s in Honduras, I did some correspondence work with the *contras* along a stretch of Honduran-Nicaraguan border known as *El Camino de los Muertos*—The Road of The Dead. The thin strip of ruts that ran between Cifuentes and Las Trojes was known as the most dangerous seventeen kilometers in the world. Las Trojes near the end of the road was a frontier town where *hombres* carried pistols thrust in their belts and *contras* from the camps in the hills beyond trickled down to trade American-supplied food for cigarettes. Uprooted by the border fighting, *desplazados*—displaced persons—haunted the wide unpaved streets of the village with fear and wariness in their eyes.

I was with a Honduran outpost along the road. A 6$^{th}$ Battalion soldier, only 17-years-old, was shot and killed by Sandinistas when he ventured from our trench emplacement to answer a call of nature. The next night, Sandinistas attacked across the border.

An explosion strobed like lightning across the dark sky and made the ground rumble. Shaken from a fitful sleep, I crowded into the trench with the Hondurans as the sudden rattle of machine gun and small arms fire rocked the valley. Excited Spanish crackled from the radio; the outpost down the road from us was being attacked.

"Keep a sharp eye," a young sergeant said. "We will be next."

"Ojalo que no, por Dios," someone prayed.

"Do not call in God's name," said another. "God does not listen to soldiers."

An hour later came a sudden warning yelp. *"They are coming!"*

The entire outpost of six soldiers opened up with a fusillade that streamed tracers across the road and cut through grass like a scythe. Panic set in. The Hondurans scrambled out the back side of the trench. Screaming and firing back over their shoulders, they bolted toward a distant tree line on top of the hill where the sergeant had established an alternate defensive position.

Not to be left behind, I joined the confusion of shadows in the night. Running, *running*. Muzzle fire blossomed. Rifles banging on full automatic. Yelling and screaming.

I completed a 40-second dash across a rising field to the tree line. Adrenaline coursed through my veins. It was like my feet never touched ground. I raced blindly through the darkness, hoping to avoid flying bullets. I had myopic vision. I threw back my head. My arms pumped.

Wham!

One moment I was running as if the Holy Roller devil from the Oklahoma hills was hot on my butt. The next moment that butt met ground with a shock that jarred my brain stem. I grabbed my face; it went instantly numb.

I gagged on blood, retched. Fingers touched mangled flesh and mustache dripping with blood and teeth barely hanging from gums. *Oh, my God! They've shot off my face!*

I lost a couple of teeth and added some scars, but I made it back. A ricochet or a rock fragment had caught me in the mouth. It was an instance in which curiosity almost killed the cat. Nonetheless, the incident failed to stifle my curiosity. My experiences from those days are included in at least four published books and probably 50 magazine articles. Now they're being included in this book.

One day, I suspect, God will reach down, grab me by the scruff of the neck, and say, "Hey, boy. Your curiosity has gone far enough. You've had enough personal experiences to last several lifetimes."

"Yes, Sir. That's what I intended. Sir, what's this I hear about heaven? I'd sure like to find out for myself. Maybe write a book...?"

# CHAPTER FOURTEEN

Few ideas come from a shallow mind, as little water comes from a shallow well. While curiosity might be the cornerstone of ideas, reading is what deepens the well of ideas. Had Aunt Ellen not given me books when she did, had I not learned the joy and value of reading to whet my inborn thirst for knowledge, I sometimes think I might still be back in the Ozarks without real purpose and goals. As it is, I read literally everything. Books, magazines, billboards, the ingredients listed on the backs of Jell-O packets.

One summer when I was nine or ten we moved into a four-room house out in the fields on Drake's Prairie. The owners, the Barneses, went to California to seek work and left three of the four rooms to us. They stored all their stuff in the fourth room and locked the door. In peeping through the key hole, curious about what was inside, I spotted a box full of paperback books. What a treasure trove! I had to get to them somehow.

Finally, I discovered a way. The high, small window at the back of the house was unlocked. I shimmied up the drain pipe and crawled through the window. I got out one book at a time, read it, returned it, selected another, without anyone ever becoming the wiser. I read every book in the box. They were mostly westerns—Zane Grey, Max Brand... *Santa Fe Trail; Silver; Tall In The Saddle...*

I had a favorite place to read out in the woods by a pond—a large blackjack oak whose limbs sagged and touched the ground to form a kind of grotto hidden from the world. I would slip away from home and crawl into my hiding place with a book, a jar of water or Kool-Aid, and a biscuit-and-jelly and read all day long. The first lesson reading teaches, said Jonathan Franzen (*How To Be Alone: Essays)*, is how to be alone. It is something a writer needs to master early.

"Learn to enjoy your own company," advised former Texas Governor Ann Richards. "You are the one person you can count on living with for the rest of your life."

I began building a "library" out of the ten or twelve books in the box Aunt Ellen gave me. I catalogued them according to subject matter, fiction and nonfiction, and arranged them alphabetically. Hemingway's *For Whom The Bell Tolls* still has on its spine the number "1", designating it the first book in my library by virtue of its being my favorite novel. Those pitiful few used books have today grown into a true library containing hundreds of volumes; it is as large as many school libraries or those in small towns.

When I was a homicide detective I had occasion while on a case to visit the home of a prominent politician. While I waited in his large library, stocked floor to ceiling with books encased in beautiful walnut shelves, I naturally browsed. To my surprise and consternation, the spines of none of those wonderful books had been broken. They had never been read. They were for show, like paintings on the walls that were never looked at.

My books are read and used, with dog-eared pages and underlinings and notes in the margins. A book is a useless thing unless opened.

In 1996, Donna Sue and I built a lovely two-story house on a ranch we own with Donna Sue's son Darren, who lives in the original ranch house with his wife Summer. High on a hill populated by pecan and oak, it overlooks an enormous pond and a sweeping, open meadow where my horses graze. The back of the ranch bumps up against Lake Fort Gibson and Flat Rock Creek. The top floor of the house has a guest room at one end and an office for Donna Sue and me at the other. Separating them at the top of the stairs is what everyone refers to as "the library and museum."

In addition to the floor-to-ceiling bookcases jammed with books, the museum contains mementos and souvenirs from my many years of banging around the world: a piranha jaw and a blowgun from the Amazon; a lynx pelt from Alaska; old bronc-riding spurs, clown "baggies," and a lariat from my early rodeo days; wood carvings from Jamaica, Central America, Africa, Korea, Thailand...; playbooks from when I've played dinner theater—*The Odd Couple; The Foreigner; Second Time Around...;* various awards and plaques; a rustic homemade oar from Mexico; bear, elk and caribou skins; a silver *reale* coin from Sir Francis Drake's treasure; a mammoth tooth carving from Alaska; a bullfight poster from Barcelona; a manikin wearing my Army Special Forces uniform; wine bottles from Germany, France, Denmark, Spain and elsewhere; the rib bone of a whale; a sea lion skull; a mounted bass and pheasant; a painting by the murderer from my book *At Large*; an abalone shell from Cedros Island; a peacock egg; a cuckoo clock from the Black Forest; Anasazi pottery shards; jade rock from a mountain on the Yukon; quilts my mom made for me; an autographed homemade rocking chair from Louisiana; shark teeth from the Gulf; my Ka-bar combat knife from Vietnam; paratrooper helmet and boots and the handle of a reserve parachute from when I had a malfunction; framed photographs and oil paintings; wooden shoes from Holland; camel hair from Egypt; a broken ski from when I first learned; petrified wood from the Smokey Mountains of Tennessee; a knitted poodle bottle warmer given to me by the daughter of "Ma and Pa Kettle" from *The Egg And I* fame...

Books are arranged library-style and cover virtually every subject. What do I read? Eclectic. Edgar Rice Burroughs' *Tarzan* series; Zane Grey; Dusty Richards; Louis L'Amour; Homer; Faulkner; Steinbeck; Hemingway; John Irving; Dean Koontz; Tom Clancy; Pat Conroy; James Clavell; Ayn Rand; Stephen King; Tad Williams; Isaac Asimov; Susan Elizabeth Phillips; Judith Henry Wall; Peggy Fielding; Jean Hager; William Bernhardt; Crystal Stovall; Johnny Quarles; Jim Stovall...

Classics, romance, science fiction, westerns, adventure, suspense, fantasy...

Nonfiction runs the same broad spectrum of my interests. I write on many different subjects; I therefore read widely. I like biographies; true adventure; philosophy; social works; politics; histories, especially of the Vietnam War and the Hitler era; how-to; religion; anthropology and archaeology; parapsychology; psychology; crime…

Halibut fishing off the coast of Alaska (center, with stocking cap). Wife Donna Sue is to my right. Her son Darren is on the far right. Les Cobb, about whom I wrote in my book *Arctic Homestead*, is to Donna Sue's right.

Slouching Toward Gomorrah by Robert H. Bork; The Book of Virtues by William J. Bennett; Illiberal Education by Dinesh D'Souza; Rousseau And Revolution by Will and Ariel Durant; The Way Things Ought To Be by Rush Limbaugh; Jesse Jackson and The Politics of Race by Thomas Landess and Richard Quinn; The Kinder, Gentler Military by Stephanie Gutmann; The Oak and The Calf by Aleksandr Solzhenitsyn; Steinbeck, A Life in Letters by Elaine Steinbeck; I Married Adventure by Osa Johnson; George and Laura: Portrait of An American Marriage by Christopher Anderson; How The Mind Works by Steven

Pinker; War Story by Jim Morris; Doorway To Hell by General
Ed Wheeler and Craig Roberts...

I like Kevin Dockery; John Weisman; David Hackworth; Bill
Fawcett; Harold Bloom; James Bovard...

After I was wounded on *El Camino de los Muertos*, I made
my way back to Tegucigalpa. It wouldn't do for the Honduran
police to catch me. No telling how long they might keep me
while I tried to explain all the blood. Besides, Americans were
not supposed to be slipping back and forth across the border with
the *contras*. I could be held in-country for weeks, months even,
while the Honduran government and the U.S. embassy worked
through red tape.

Racked with chills and fever, I made my way through the
city's nighttime shadows. Latin American cities are almost always dark. I came at last to Ana's house, a pleasant little pastel
adobe jammed close to the street with a courtyard in back. It sat
in the dark with no light in the window. I shot glances to right
and left, then rapped on the door.

A sleepy female voice. "*Quien es?*"

"Es Carlos, Ana. Tengo dano."

"What?"

"I have difficulty talking. I am wounded. Ana? Ana, it is me.
Carlos."

The door flew open. Ana stood there with her dark hair flying and her face pale in the thin silver moonlight. Ana's family
was Castilian, Old Spain. Light olive skin, eyes gray rather than
dark. Her face clouded with sudden dread when she saw the
blood on my khaki shirt.

"I'm hurt, Ana. I didn't know where else to go."

She grabbed me, hugged me, blood and filth and all. Ana
could get me out of the country. She worked for a travel agency.
That was how we met on one of my previous trips to Honduras.

"I thought I was dying," I said.

"You cannot die, Carlos. I want to keep you."

I stayed with Ana while I recuperated enough to leave the
country. My lips were shredded; a doctor friend of Ana's

stitched the wounds. I had lost teeth and weight. I looked into the mirror to shave and saw a face bloated and turned hideous in shades of green and red and purple.

"You are a beautiful man where it counts most—inside," Ana said. "I see that in you when you let me. *Que tu quieres, chico?*"

"Nothing. I want nothing."

"We all must want something in order to get it."

Outside Ana's bedroom grew a lime tree. Its thin limbs scratched against the window when there was a breeze. Scratching like the dry bones of a corpse risen in the sun. It was sobering. I could have been killed along the road called *El Camino de los Muertos*.

While I recuperated, I read *Don Quixote*, laboring over it. It was one of my favorite novels. I had always wanted to read it in the original Spanish.

# # #

I belong to a number of book clubs, including Writer's Digest, Doubleday, Equine, Conservative, Military, and Paperback Book Club. I subscribe to daily newspapers and magazines ranging from *Western Horseman, Reader's Digest* and *Odyssey* to *Biblical Archaeology, Outdoor Photography* and *National Review*. I purchase books, papers and magazines covering a broad spectrum of political and social issues, from the far Left to the far Right. I rarely watch TV, that vast wasteland, except for Fox News, History Channel, Friday Night Fights, and an occasional movie. From my reading, as well as from other sources, I take notes on ideas for future books or magazine pieces and stockpile them in file folders.

My file folders at this moment contain ideas for books on: shrunken heads; the 761st Tank Battalion in World War II; poverty; a small town cop; a CIA agent in Turkey; a counterterrorist FBI agent; eleven black GI's executed by the Nazi SS during the Battle of The Bulge; cattle rustling; taxes; new novels about the war on terror and the Iraqi war...

They include ideas for magazine articles on: the battle for Okinawa; a "pig drive" to Kansas; how "ugly girls" were hired for school teachers in the Old West because cowboys kept marrying the pretty ones; freedom of the press as voiced by the colonists; a chiropractor for horses; old farms; the "war against Christianity;" my record-breaking transcontinental flight in a powered parachute; political correctness in writing...

More ideas than I can ever hope to use. Yet, I constantly add to them. In selecting ideas for filing, I'm guided by such considerations as whether I have strong feelings for or against something; by current events and by changes in the mores and manners of society; by new inventions and social upheavals; and by my own varied personal tastes and interests. When I complete one project, I immediately go to my files for the next. The files continue to produce books and many, many articles.

> Exactly what brought an end to the Southwestern culture known to archaeologists as the Pueblo Tradition remains a mystery. What *is* known is that the original farming civilizations that constructed elaborate multi-story towns and controlled much of the Four Corner states of Colorado, Utah, Arizona, and New Mexico for over 600 years now lies beneath time and dust—along with the treasures they accumulated...
>
> Today, their property, found in abundance in many sites, is considered fine art and commands astounding prices on the world market. Interest in Southwestern Indian artifacts appears especially strong among German and Japanese collectors...
>
> "The Alien Ancient Ones," *Lost Treasure*

In addition to "idea files," I also maintain "clip files." Each day I go through newspapers and magazines scissoring out what interests me and what *may* interest me at some point. I then file according to subject matter. The cabinets in my office are stuffed with tabbed file folders under at least 20 different headings, such as *Terrorism, Politics, Crime, Space, Adventure, War...*

I began clipping years ago while writing crime stories for true detective publications. Ghoulish as it may sound, I scanned the local and regional dailies for new murders. I filed the clippings under the name of the murder victim and maintained it from the time the crime was committed until suspects were caught, convicted and sentenced, thereby allowing me to write the piece. I even sold an article, the cover feature, for *Writer's Digest* on how to write true crime.

> Most true crime magazines focus on murder. A true murder mystery is as timely as the morning newspaper headlines and as enduring as human curiosity. It is a real story about real people caught up in a situation that grows progressively more suspenseful until the local cop knocks down the suspect's front door...
> "Making Crime Pay," *Writer's Digest*

Gradually, I began keeping files on other topics that interested me. For example, when the phenomena we now call "political correctness" swept America, I opened a file that eventually grew into an entire cabinet full of materials. So far, that data has produced a half-dozen magazine articles, a novel *(Liberty City*, AmErica House, 2000), and a nonfiction book, *Going Bonkers: The Wacky World of Cultural Madness.*

My clip files also helped generate at least two true crime books—*Homicide!* (Pocket Books, 1990) and *At Large* (St. Martin's, 1998). *At Large* and I were featured on the popular *America's Most Wanted* TV series.

My book *Smoke Jumpers* (Pocket Books, 1996) came about largely as a result of a magazine article I read about these daring souls who parachute into forest fires to put them out. I clipped and filed. The file grew and grew over the next year or so until it demanded release in a book and several magazine articles.

> "They wouldn't dare send us to hell. We'd put it out."
> Smokejumpers, elite firefighters who parachute out of the sky to battle forest fires in the American West, have adopted this saying as somewhat of a proverb, a summation of who they are and what they do.

When a fire starts high on a ridge, deep in the backcountry, fire management officers summon the elite smokejumpers to contain the blaze before it escalates and threatens lives and property. Only 350-strong nationally, they are the Special Forces of wildland firefighters, trained as an immediate reaction force to parachute into the heart of a spreading fire, extinguish the inferno or hold the line until the infantry ground troops arrive...

"Smokejumpers," *Adventure West*

In the year 2000, the destroyer USS *Cole* was bombed by terrorists in the port of Aden, Yemen, killing seventeen American sailors. I used that incident juxtaposed against world politics and military operations to launch my fictional series about a U.S. Army Delta Force detachment sent on missions to combat worldwide terrorism. *(Detachment Delta: Punitive Strike,* Avon 2002; *Detachment Delta: Operation Iron Weed,* Avon 2003; *Detachment Delta: Operation Deep Steel,* Avon 2004). I pulled my "idea files" and my "clip files" and used them to work into my copy that extra taste of reality and authenticity.

My editor, Jennifer Fisher, received the first *Delta* manuscript five days before the 9-11 terrorist attack on New York and the Pentagon. She wrote me back four days after the attack. "There was an eerie sense of wondering what was fact and what was fiction," she said.

See what I mean about reading and ideas and maintaining files? The well is always full of ideas if you dig it deep enough.

# CHAPTER FIFTEEN

While curiosity is the cornerstone of ideas and reading deepens the well of ideas, it is observation—paying attention to what is seen, heard, touched, smelled, tasted, then having the dexterity to recall or imagine these feelings and sensations—that provides not only ideas but also improves the writer's ability to record these ideas and the world they represent so that others may experience them as well. I like to go out walking early whenever I am in a strange place. I walk the streets of cities—Paris, Barcelona, Bangkok, Lima, Seattle—and I walk seashores, forests, mountains. What I'm doing is *observing*. For it is through close observation of the world around us, through watching people, nature, weather, sunsets and sunrises, the progress of a lady bug along a leaf, a flight of Canadian honkers winging south, that our sensations tell us we are truly alive. That we are *living*.

Long after an experience, I can still close my eyes and feel it, see it, re-live it. I feel the salty chill in the morning breeze off the Gulf of Mexico as an old friend and I prepare for shark fishing— the shriek of gulls as they dive for bait fish; the way the red orb of the sun pops up from the watery horizon; the mixed smell of salt air and engine exhaust and iced beer. I feel the excitement of laying the rod into the big fish and the way it seemed the bottom of the ocean came up and grabbed the chunk of bait and took off with it. The way the line stung and cut my fingers as it sang off the reel.

> The shark's jaws snapped open and you could see the vicious rows of teeth and the eyes like a dead cobra's. Rain pelted the seas, and the seas crashed against the boat. We were dragging the anchor. The boat listed coming up out of the troughs. Seas slammed across the stern and for a moment we were knee deep in salt water.
>
> I thought we were sinking.
> "Don't cut the line."

Gubbins was coughing. He slung water from the pistol barrel.

"She'll be in the boat with us," he shouted above the fury and the excitement. "Or we'll be with her."

"Gubbins, shoot her. Now!"

"This Bud's for you," Gubbins said. He thrust the pistol at the shark and shot her in her small brain.

She went mad. It only lasted a second. I strained hard on the rod against the last of the shark's fight. Her tail thrashed and she tried to dive through a wave tinged with her own blood. She turned belly up. The storm thudded her against the side of the boat...

"Keepers," *Read Me*

We must first be aware of sensations in ourselves in order to stimulate the reader's sensations. The writer not only lives experiences, he or she observed them and analyzes them. Poet e.e. cummings characterized himself as a "wily observer of everything under the sun." Writing, he said, requires acute observational skills. The development of "true-seeming" plots, of authentic and "real" prose, depends upon a wide knowledge of not only how others respond to words, gestures, events, but also how we feel and respond to them and to our surroundings.

Novelist Daphne Du Maurier (*The Flight of The Falcon; Jamaica's Inn*) recalls when she first realized the relationship between observation and writing and how she became aware of living on two different planes, one on which she participated, the other on which she observed.

"Somewhere, buried in the unconscious of the eighteen-year-old, must have been the embryo writer observing, watching..." she wrote. "The seed of an idea, sorting itself from others, might take some five and twenty years or more to germinate and come to the surface, fusing with later observations, these observations in turn blending with characters from long-forgotten books, but finally a story or a novel would emerge."

Her autobiographical-like volumes are filled with events that she saw and stored away in her memory to use later as details in her novels. Her teenage crush on the much-older Basil Rathbone came out in *Rebecca*. A ship disaster near her home provided the flavor and part of the plot of *Manderley*.

Shark fishing in the Gulf of Mexico.

Sometimes it doesn't take much to stimulate the imagination. The beautiful woman on the bus in El Salvador with her big rough hands, the scent of a high mountain breeze soughing through pines... Tennessee Williams said *A Streetcar Named De-*

*sire* originated from a single image. "I simply had the vision of a woman in her late youth. She was sitting on a chair all alone by a window with the moonlight streaming in on her desolate face, and she'd been stood up by the man she planned to marry."

I often draw characters and settings from my own observations and experiences. Growing up on farms and in fields harvesting crops and roaming the Ozarks left indelible impressions. I see even now my grandfather in his overalls and old felt hat and one stiff bad finger sticking out, standing in the ploughed field behind the old brown mule Jude, drinking from a quart fruit jar held up against the sun. Water trickling down the seams at the corners of his mouth make clean paths on his dusty chin and leave dark drops on the drying upturned earth. I taste the cool well water when Pa passes the jar to me, see my grandmother standing there waiting with her hands on her hips, only two teeth left in her mouth, one on one side, one on the other, so that she has to slide her jaw to one side to set the two teeth into the roll-yer-own cigarette to hold it.

> In the fields the green spears of corn shot up, and the tender cotton, and the truck garden crops. The corn was best to watch mature. It spread its leaves and opened flat blades to the sun. Later, the blades browned on the edges and gossiped and rattled whenever the wind blew. Then there was food on the stalks. It was a cycle familiar to us on the farm. From the fallow field came waving infant green which gave way to stalks of food torn from the heart and guts of the plowed earth, and then, after the last plowing, once more the fallow land...
> "Jeremiad," South Dakota Review

Somerset Maugham believed it was "essential for a writer unceasingly to study men." Not only their physical appearances, but also their behavior. "You must be ready to listen for hours to the retelling of second-hand information in order at last to catch the hint or the casual remark that betrays."

Dorothy Canfield Fisher said she needed to experience what she wrote in order to write well. "I can write nothing," she said, "if I cannot achieve these very definite, very complete visualizations of the scenes; which means that I can write nothing at all about places, people or phases of life which I do not intimately know, down to the last detail."

The patience to look and look again, said Pablo Picasso, is a trait that characterizes great artists. That gift of observation might be detected in two people who walk across town together. One merely moves from one location to the other, having only destination in mind. The other, brighter-brained, observes and senses all through which he passes, making use of all his senses—hearing, seeing, tasting, feeling, smelling. He consciously maintains a child-like wonder and curiosity in the world around him. He literally absorbs the world through his senses and, if he is a writer, stores it all away for later use. My friends often chide each other to watch out, because I'll steal their lives and write about them.

Stephen King may be the most underestimated novelist of our generation. *The Stand* was pure genius. His use of observational skills in his horror and suspense novels is what moves the reader from the mundane, the normal, to the unthinkable, the inconceivable. In *Pet Semetery*, he takes an ordinary event like a semi-truck running over a cat and transforms it into pure terror. You see the brown autumn leaves blowing in the suburban streets of a typical American small town, and the leaves reappear in the spring, as the cat is resurrected. You know, you *know,* that the little boy is going to die too and come back—with a few changes.

Poet Herbert Read thinks Observation is "almost entirely an acquired skill. It is true that certain individuals are born with an aptitude for concentrated attention, and for the eye-and-hand co-ordination involved in the act of recording what is observed. But in most cases the eye (and the other organs of sensation) have to be trained, both in observation and notation."

Observation is a skill in which the more you invest, the more it returns. It is a skill that can be learned, improved, or fine-turned through practice. It is not be accident that so many poets and novelists have had training in the visual arts—William Blake, William Thackeray, Thomas Hardy, the Bronte sisters; Henry Miller, J.R.R. Tolkein...

All writers are admonished to write about what they know. While it is a sage piece of advice, I would add to it to prevent restrictions. Write about what you know, to be sure, but if you want to write about a particular subject or locale of which you are temporarily ignorant, then go out and observe and learn about it so that you *do* know.

I fell in love with wild Alaska. Caribou hunting on the rolling tundra, down along the streams furred with willow and back up through stunted spruce where there are moose. I sometimes tramp many miles during each day's hunt. Not so much seeking game to shoot as taking in all this wild free country, absorbing it. I *knew* Alaska when it came time to write a book about it.

A friend of mine, Les Cobb, is an Alaskan big game guide. Les, his wife Norma and their five children, the youngest of which were one-year-old twins, pulled up stakes in the Lower 48 in 1973 and headed north to Alaska to follow a pioneer dream of claiming land. The only land available lay north of Fairbanks near the Arctic Circle where grizzlies outnumbered humans 20 to one. By a convoluted set of circumstances they became the last pioneers to sign up under the U.S. Homestead Act. On top of its fierce winters and predatory animals, the Alaskan frontier also drew the more unsavory elements of society's fringes. The Cobbs found themselves pitted against nature, wild animals, and unscrupulous bandits who would rob from new settlers, shoot them, burn them out, or jump their claims.

In the book I wrote about the Cobb family, I told the story first-person through Norma's point of view. I had observed her and her family over several summers and falls hunting and fishing with them, hanging out at Lost Creek Ranch, and once helping Les move a string of horses 150 miles across the wilderness to a hunting camp. This was my first attempt at writing from a woman's point of view.

Even the children stopped eating. Early October's first snowfall murmured in the darkness against the spruce log cabin. Silence fell around the table, so that the fire in the wood-burning oil drum roared like a grizzly coming down the stovepipe and the whisper of snow on the black windows became as ominous as gossip at a funeral wake.

The way Les looked at me, half apologetically, half triumphantly... Panic leered from shadows resurrected to life by the uncertain flicker of the oil lamp. Tears blurred my vision. It wasn't as though I hadn't known tonight or a night like tonight eventually had to come. Sometimes I blocked from my mind things I didn't want to happen. I didn't trust myself to speak. I knew I might say things I surely would come to regret in hindsight. The hush built...

*Arctic Homestead* (with Norma Cobb, St. Martin's, 2000)

How well did I incorporate my observations into the story? Look at the critics' reviews.

"Cobb's voice combines the ruggedness of the frontier with the tenderness of a caring mother, resulting in an appealing, and enjoyable quick read."—*Publishers Weekly.*

"Her story exhibits her strength and sheer willpower to make it work."—*The Oregonian.*

"Turn off the TV, throw a log on the fire, unpack your dreams. This is the real thing: a farewell account of our greatest myth about ourselves, the frontier myth. Norma Cobb writes with a skinning knife and gun stock, with bear grease and shards of river ice—a memoir as wild, engaging, stubborn, and authentic as that distant valley where her family staked out the last plot in America."—John Balzar, author of *Yukon Alone.*

Failure to use observational skills can be crippling to the writer. Some writers are well up in grammar and the craft of writing, in communications and analysis, but nonetheless remain destitute of ideas because they fail to develop and exercise feel-

ing, empathizing, observing, and other ways of knowing reality
directly. Thinkers learn to translate ideas generated by these
"tools of thinking" into writing to express their insights.

Bear hunting in Canada.

Virginia Woolf's father wanted to be a novelist, but his skills at human observation and understanding remained undeveloped throughout his life. As Virginia noted, he could produce nothing creative beyond dry, analytical criticism.

"Give him a thought to analyze," she said, and his writing was "acute, clear, concise... But give him life, a character, and he is so crude, so elementary, so conventional, that a child with a box of coloured chalks is as subtle a portrait painter as he."

He never published a novel.

"He was almost completely isolated," Virginia said of his last years. "Whole traits of his sensibility had atrophied. He had so ignored, or refused to face, or disguised his own feelings, that not only had he no conception of what he himself did or said, he had no idea of what other people felt."

# CHAPTER SIXTEEN

The most important tools for digging your well of ideas deep are curiosity, reading, observation, and imagination. Ideas flourish with deep thought, with introspection and time spent alone getting to know yourself while you let your imagination run wild. As a kid, I must have absolutely driven my dad nuts. He was a practical man, close to earth with a small head and big hands, and as narrow as one of the furrows we plowed into Oklahoma hardpan. I was his opposite. Not only did I always have a book stuck somewhere nearby but I was also always daydreaming. While my body might have been in those cotton fields, my thoughts were building castles in the sky. In my imagination I traveled all over the world, jousting to win the hands of pretty maidens, waging battles single-handedly (like Don Quixote?), climbing mountains, crossing oceans. At various times I was Tarzan, Jungle Jim, the Lone Ranger, Sergeant Preston of the Yukon, Jack London on the *Snark*, Roy Rogers, Buck Rogers... I had wonderful adventures. Naturally, I was always the hero.

"If he don't have his nose stuck in a damned book, he's got his head in the clouds," Dad complained.

Two of my most influential heroes were Martin and Osa Johnson. Throughout the early 1900s, this husband and wife team explored the remote corners of the world, filming 16mm movies which they showed to sell-out crowds around the United States. I always dreamed that one day I would meet a girl like Osa who would share my adventures.

Martin sailed with Jack London around the world on the *Snark* when he was only sixteen. He met Osa in his own home state of Kansas during one of his film-showing tours. They got married and together set out exploring and adventuring until Martin died in an airplane crash in 1935. Osa wrote a book, *I Married Adventure* (J.B. Lippincott, 1940). I read it so many times I almost wore it out. The Foreword spurred my imagination with: "Martin was as born to adventure as Leif-The-Lucky, and when Osa married Martin she married his destiny too. It was to be always a-going, always a-seeing. Home was to be a schooner in the South Seas, a raft in Borneo, a tent on safari, a hunt in the black Congo, sometimes a dash to Paris, interludes of an apartment on Fifth Avenue—but always a place to be going from..."

I *was* Martin Johnson all the way through high school. I transformed the Ozarks in my imagination into the jungles of Borneo; my dogs and I fought more than one pitched battle against headhunters. I loved to ride the school bus because it gave me an hour all to myself morning and afternoon to gaze out the window and daydream. Just like Martin, I traveled all over the world during these sessions. Martin filmed his adventures; I wrote about them. I was building a myth in my mind of what I would do and what I would become. If the imagination can conceive it, I read somewhere, the mind can achieve it.

I still like to drive long distances when I can just drive and drive and let my daydreams go. If you cannot imagine, you cannot create.

"Illusion is first of all needed to find the powers of which the self is capable," wrote Paul Horgan, Pulitzer prize-winning author. "If you can't conceive of things that don't exist, you can't create anything new. If you can't dream up worlds that might be, then you are limited to the worlds other people describe."

Flying and space has always intrigued me. As a kid back in the hills, I often hiked to the bluffs on Wild Horse Mountain overlooking the Arkansas River. It was almost like flying if I stood with my toes stuck out over the edge. The mountain dropped down sheer for several hundred feet, leveled off, then plunged again successively until it fell into the brown river nearly a thousand feet below and several miles away. I stood as close to the edge as I could and tilted back my head until all I saw were sky and clouds and maybe a hawk riding a thermal over the river.

I *became* that hawk, trimming a wing feather, circling, soaring, hunting. I spread my wings and felt the wind tearing across them. I chandelled and dived and swooped, standing there as close as I could to the edge of the cliff.

Hunting caribou in Alaska.

I became a private airplane pilot years later, just as I had imagined in my youth. I earned my license while I was in Florida. I loved to fly alone in a Cessna 150 out over the Everglades, low and fast, buzzing the alligators.

In the navy, I was offered the opportunity to fly for the military under the NavCad program; I turned it down only because I had a bigger dream of becoming a writer. I also almost won the opportunity to fly NASA's space shuttle among the stars, and I still haven't given up that hope. I became a paratrooper with Army Special Forces. Jumping out of an aircraft in flight and slowly sailing to earth was almost like being that hawk I used to see riding the gentle winds above the Arkansas River. I spent 13 years as a paratrooper.

Lightning. A bolt of raw electricity strobed, crackling in the night clouds beyond the slipstream roaring past the open paratroop doors of the C-130 Hercules. And I saw Central America... Panama below through the open doors—the black of jungle without relief, the ocean reflecting back the lightning in quick mirror return...

Rain skittered and beaded on the metal aircraft floor. The airplane bounced in the storm. During another bolt of lightning, Mother Norman cast a quick glance along the stick of paratroopers waiting for the signal. Then it was dark again, and there were the jump lights throbbing red at the doors. And Felber, the jumpmaster, leaning dangerously far out into the wind searching for lights on the drop zone. Slipstream and darkness molded his face into his jump helmet.

"Sharks'll get you if you drop into the ocean," we were warned during isolation at Fort Chaffee. "Don't land in the jungle either. Jungle trees splinter, you could get one jabbed up your ass. You must hit the DZ, no matter what."

In a storm? On the darkest night? At three a.m.? Laden with one hundred pounds of battle gear each? Jumping from less than one thousand feet onto a strange DZ we couldn't even see...?

*Always A Warrior* (Pocket Books, 1994)

After I married Donna Sue, her son Darren and I began flying, and instructing other pilots to fly, powered parachutes. A powered parachute (PPC) is an ultralite aircraft that uses a parachute as a wing. Essentially, it looks like a go-cart suspended underneath a square parachute. When I was 60-years-old, I set a world's record by being the first to make a transcontinental flight in one of the strange little airplanes. I flew a Six-Chuter SR-5 PPC from San Diego, California, to St. Mary's, Georgia. It took 23 days to fly 2,400 miles at an average speed of about 26 mph.

I had heard of three or four other flyers who attempted the coast-to-coast, all of whom crashed along the way. I thought the same fate was about to befall me while flying California's coastal mountains, only an hour after I took off. Winds howled out of canyons, through rocky passes and sheered off the edges of precipes. Parachute and lines popped and snapped as I whipped violently across an angry sky. Sometimes I dropped two or three hundred feet, then was immediately jerked back up like on a roller coaster gone maniac. On occasion I was actually flying *backwards.*

Nonetheless, flying the PPC was the closest I have ever come to being that hawk. Weary but triumphant, I reached the east coast of Georgia on July 28, 2001. I followed St. Mary's River out to the Atlantic Ocean, to make the trip official from sea-to-sea, then turned back to the airport. I circled the field once, reveling in the accomplishment, reluctant to land and end it.

I made a perfect touchdown, smooth as silk. I sat in the seat grinning as news people, local ultralite pilots, my friend Darrell Turner, who was providing ground crew on this last leg, and others came running to take a look.

"You brought that thing from *where?*" one incredulous pilot asked.

Yep. All the way across America. Just like some of the daydreams conjured up in the imagination of a little hill kid standing on the edge of a cliff overlooking the Arkansas River.

I love Mark Twain. Like Tom Sawyer and Huck Finn, my brothers and I spent days designing log rafts and floating them on creeks and rivers. One year Joe and I intended to run away from home to seek our fortunes. We built a raft which we would float down Big Sallisaw Creek to the Arkansas River and then on to the Mississippi.

Although it broke apart in some fast water, I continued to daydream of constructing an elaborate raft—more of a crude houseboat in my mind—and floating it down the Mississippi just like Tom Sawyer and Huck Finn. I did exactly that when I was 36-years-old, providing my sons David and Michael and their friend David McCracken a summer's adventure they still talk about.

The boys promptly christened the raft "Huck Finn." We determined to float the currents the Huck Finn way, without any power other than oars and the current itself, taking our leisure to skinny dip, sunbathe, and explore mysterious islands for river pirate treasure...

"Huck Finning The Mississippi," Tulsa *Tribune*

In this manner, imagination has continued to turn my daydreams into eventual reality. I rented a Honda 500cc motorcycle and rode it with third wife Nita, who was my girlfriend at the time, all over England, Wales, Ireland and Scotland. I particularly wanted to see Shakespeare's birthplace, Stonehenge and Sherwood Forest, over which my imagination had gone wild in reading the stories of Robin Hood. Sadly, all that remained of Sherwood Forest is a tourist trap of about 80 acres.

I took my nephew Bobby Shaffer and a friend's sons, R.J. and Austin Ellis, to the badlands of southern Utah to search for Anasazi ruins. We backpacked in, camped on high canyon walls, and scaled or descended cliffs to reach the remnants of 1,000-year-old ruins. It was high adventure for the boys, the oldest of whom was fourteen. It was high adventure for me.

Writing and the ideas for writing can never sprout in a desert of boredom. Ideas are born and live only if the writer is *alive*. I hereby give you permission to daydream and to use your imagination to "see" things as they can be—and then turn them into reality and into print. I told my mom many years ago that I was going to live many lives and write about them. And I have.

*Writer's Yearbook 1931* asked Frances Parkinson Keyes what he considered to be the necessary ingredients from which to build a successful writer.

"One must have at least a tiny spark of that God-given flame, which we call talent," he replied, "a flexible and extensive vocabulary; a natural sense of word values and phrase forms; an aptitude for facile and rapid observation and the ability to record observations clearly and convincingly; a knowledge of human nature and an attitude of sympathetic understanding toward it; a sincerity which is so complete that, since it never permits self-deception, never fails to leave its imprint on others; a vivid imagination; a retentive memory; and an unpoisoned sense of humor..."

Artist Pablo Picasso was said to have encountered a man on a train who complained of how modern art distorts reality. Picasso demanded to know what his companion considered a faithful representation of reality. The man took out a wallet-sized photo.

"That's a real picture," he said. "That's what my wife really looks like."

Picasso looked it over carefully from several angles. Finally, he said, "She's awfully small. And flat."

Without imagination, all the world is as flat and small as that picture.

# SECTION V:
# Craft

*"There will come a day, if you persist, when your pen will move nimbly and you will feel elated, and exclaim to yourself, 'Now, I know that I can write.'"*

— *Arnold Bennett*

Starring in a dinner theater production of *Second Time Around*. (Center right, sitting, with wife Donna Sue, also starring.)

155

# CHAPTER SEVENTEEN

All writers receive rejections, even after they become successful. A piece *really* might not "meet our current needs." Perhaps it isn't the right style, or it is slanted toward the wrong audience. There is any number of other reasons why it may be rejected that has nothing to do with the quality of the writing or the author's abilities. However, *constant* rejection can mean only one thing: Your writing isn't good enough.

"People used to tell me things that were wrong with my stories and I would go cold and stony on them," Stephen King recalled. "For ten years in my twenties I couldn't get a word published and now writing dreams come true for me every day."

Many of the most successful writers are not overly burdened with talent, as we saw when I compared my modest endowments with the greater talent of my friend Ken in the navy. We should possess a modicum of it, naturally, but what we really must have is an understanding of the so-called five magic steps I talk about in this book. That includes a complete mastery of the *craft* of writing. What I call writing's nuts and bolts.

During the first hour of one of my writing classes, a student's hand shot up.

"It doesn't matter, does it, if my English is poor and my spelling awful?" he asked. "I mean, isn't that what editors are for? Writers create and put their ideas on paper and editors take care of grammar and stuff and making it read better. Right?"

Wrong.

There is a man who is a carpenter. No. There is a man who *says* he is a carpenter. He has a grand idea for a wonderful mansion he wants to build. There is only one problem. He cannot drive a nail, pour concrete, or miter a joint. He doesn't know a joist from a truss. What do you suppose his house will look like when he finishes it, *if* he finishes it? Will anyone want to buy it?

Writing, like carpentry, demands know-how. Craft. You may be as disciplined as Ghandi, as inspired as Mother Teresa, have your goal set on the moon, and be flooded with ideas, but the house you build or the novel your write will never sell unless you possess the craft to build it properly. Learning that craft is a process that continues throughout your career. The apprenticeship alone for most of us reached the length of indentured servants. There is an old joke that makes the rounds of most writers conferences. A student is seen leaving in a huff with her suitcase, exclaiming, "I've been here four days—and I'm still not published."

There is as much fact as fiction in the story. Most of us simply are not willing to endure the apprenticeship, not when you can go out tomorrow, get a *real* job, and receive a paycheck in two weeks. The rest of us—the few, the brave, the daft, perhaps—keep banging our heads against the literary wall.

"The hardest thing in the world to do is to write straight honest prose on human beings," Ernest Hemingway declared. "First, you have to know the subject; then you have to know how to write. Both take a lifetime to learn."

Particular factions within the so-called "literary community" champion the elitist view that writers are born, that they either are endowed by their Creator with talent or they are not. If not, all the sweat and tears in the world are not going to help them. Talent certainly helps, but I disagree vehemently with such a narrow premise. The craft of writing *can* be learned.

"One cannot give the writer an ear," admitted Sol Stein, noted novelist, editor and publisher. "But craft can be learned, and, surprising to some, even observation can be trained to be more acute, precise, particular."

Books and other publications on writing abound and offer an invaluable resource for both the aspiring and veteran writer. I read books on writing constantly. Some are worthless, others almost necessary. They range from the general, such as Stephen King's *On Writing* (Scribner, 2000) or David Morrell's *Lessons From A Lifetime Of Writing* (Writer's Digest Books, 2002), to the very specific, like Gary Provost's *How To Write and Sell*

*True Crime* (Writer's Digest Books, 1991) or *Writing Research Papers* by James D. Lester (Scott, Foresman & Co., 1984).

You can buy a book on how to write a novel, a short story, a romance, or how to write travel articles, greeting card verse, songs... There is a book on how to write about dog shows, another on the "art" of graffiti. I am convinced you can find a book somewhere telling you how to capture in print the romantic proclivities of the giant African toad, were you so inclined.

In addition to books, there are the various writers trade journals. Each issue of magazines like *Writers' Digest, The Writer* and *Byline* is devoted to wordsmithing. Sample issues contain hard advice pieces such as "Three Hallmarks of Style," "Putting Suspense In The Thriller," "Weave Fact Into Fiction," and "10 Dialogue Dos and Don'ts."

The journals also keep you abreast of publishing trends, markets, gossip, and other information related to the writing profession. All serious writers read them. After all, don't doctors subscribe to *The American Medical Journal* and lawyers to *The American Bar Journal?*

Other important resources are local universities, junior colleges, and recreation and civic organizations that offer classes on writing. I once taught writing for a city park department. Many of these classes are worth an investment. However, I suggest the first thing you obtain from a prospective advisor or instructor is his credentials. Be wary of anyone who proposes to advise or to teach the writing craft when his total publishing credits consist of three articles in something like *The Plains Casket Workers Journal* and a poem in *The Possum Trot Sentinel.* Such a person teaching you how to write a best-selling novel is a bit like our carpenter who has built two dog houses and a chicken coop now endeavoring to teach you how to build the Sistine Chapel. Want to bet on the outcome?

Also available in nearly every town or city are writers clubs that offer seminars and critique groups. Here again, as with courses in writing, you have to approach them with a built-in BS detector. Learn to take what works for you and discard the rest.

When I suggested to one novice writer that he join a writers club, his first predictable response was, "I want to be a *professional* writer. I don't want to be part of a group of amateurs who meet every other Tuesday for coffee and gossip."

Some writer's clubs *are* sewing circles. However, a good writer's club offers a combination of support, encouragement, inspiration, social outlet and learning opportunity. You can always tell the better ones. Their memberships include selling professionals as well as beginners. Here, you meet people in publishing. You obtain access to seminars, workshops, and critique groups that can help you master the very difficult skills of writing professionally.

A good writers club also reassures you that you are not, as I once supposed, utterly alone.

# # #

One of the best ways to learn about writing, I have always maintained, is to read. Craft evolves out of a love of reading and the printed word. It is not enough, however, to simply love literature if you aspire to spend your life as a scribbler. In order to learn and sharpen your skills, you must read not only for enjoyment but also with a critical eye and ear for narrative, dialogue, transitions, suspense, character development, scene building and the other "carpenter's tools" of the trade. Look at the overall effect of a novel, book, article, or short story, then dissect it down to bones and sinews and see how it all goes together. Read to see how an author creates a particular mood, effects a scene. Read to see what he did—or failed to do—in constructing the finished product.

Read.

Plotting and the use of suspense techniques took me nearly 30 years to understand and apply. I must have written a hundred novels and either burned them or stuffed them into a drawer before I understood the concept. My novels were always "about this cop, see, who works a black ghetto," or "about this guy, see, who goes to Africa and has all kinds of adventures." Plotting, which is story telling, which is the foundation of writing, is not *about* something. It is a very precise concept. Kazan might have best expressed it when he said it was like two dogs fighting over a bone.

Someone wants something very badly. Something or someone else prevents his getting it. He must overcome all kinds of obstacles in order to obtain it.

What took me so long to utilize that simple skill? All I know is that I began selling books when I finally understood. *No Gentle Streets* was the first novel in which I comprehended my craft and applied it. I may not have applied it well, but it was the best I could do at the time. In this novel, I learned the most essential skill of all: How to designated the bone over which my characters would struggle.

In the book, Homicide Detective Harry Rawls is obsessed with finding a serial killer. He is losing his own wife and family in the process.

Their first years together had been the good years, Rawls remembered. He was working uniform patrol then, and all a uniform man had to worry about was one watch at a time. It was a simple, direct life in a rough, rowdy, brawling sort of way. Prowling dark alleys and busting up bar fights and chasing burglars. Kick ass and take names and pictures. One day at a time. He didn't have any Gerry Mobley and Hope Reynolds and Susan Olliver cases to take home with him then. The uniform job, compared to that of a detective, put a man under relatively little pressure.

The young brawny cops and their pretty wives got together at cops' bars and danced, and the girls bragged about their big, rough lawmen, and the patrolmen swapped outrageous lies about gunfights and high speed chases and hypes and cross-eyed whores. They laughed a lot. The cops. The wives. Margie. And Rawls.

"Something happened to you after you killed that man and went upstairs to C.I.D.," Margie complained. "You stopped laughing. I don't like for you to work Homicide. You see dead bodies every day. When you come home you talk about dead bodies. It's affected you, Harry. It isn't healthy working with dead people so much."

*No Gentle Streets* (Ashley Books, 1984)


The novel was unabashedly autobiographical, as, I suppose, are all first novels. It sold very modestly indeed. I am content that it disappear forever, poor writing and all. In it I opened my heart and spilled out blood in a way that embarrasses me now and reminds me of a quote by Harlan Ellison.

"(Writing) is a dangerous undertaking at the most primitive level," he wrote. "For, it seems to me, the art of writing with serious intent involved enormous personal risk. You open your soul to the world and hope no one stomps all over it. You open your soul to yourself and hope you learn no truths about yourself that are too terrible to bear."

One day, years after *No Gentle Streets* had gone out of print, I was doing a book signing when a fan appeared with a copy from *Amazon.com*. He said he paid $800 for it because he wanted a complete collection of all my books. While flattered, I was nonetheless embarrassed that he would be reading it.

I wrote and published several nonfiction books before I attempted another novel. I was much more skilled by then. *The 100^{th} Kill* is a good book that remained in print for ten years and is about to be released again. Although the story itself was complex, the plot line was simple: In Vietnam, a young sniper with a past strives to become the most successful sniper in history by killing 100 enemy soldiers. A journalist telling the story is the protagonist.


Dog started to walk off with the rifle hanging from the end of his arm...

"Sir, do you know who Pablo Rhoades is?"

"He was a sniper. I understand he's in a hospital in Japan now."

"Pablo had ninety-three kills before the gooks fried him in an Ontos, an amphibious track. During one mission he low-crawled on his belly across an open field just like this one in order to kill an NVA general. It took him three days to crawl one thousand meters."

He looked back over his shoulder with those bleached eyes.

"I'm going to get one hundred kills," he said.

*The 100$^{th}$ Kill* (Pocket Books, 1992)

# # #

Finally, you learn writing as you learn anything else—by *doing.* You learn the rules, the skills, and then you practice them by applying posterior to chair and working each day to do the best you can. You learn to avoid the beginner's nemesis of overwriting. You learn to be concise, precise, and you learn how to grab your reader with a first sentence, how to twist a dramatic phrase or hammer out a startling but satisfying conclusion. You grasp the concept and the use of such tools as "tagging," "fore-shadowing," "flashback," and "plants." If you don't understand these words, you need to do more study. And you learn how to study markets and slant for them.

Improvement, mastery of craft, comes only through application of it. Hammering and sawing, if you will. In spite of his modesty, Edgar Rice Burroughs, author of the *Tarzan* series, knew his craft and said he improved by striving to do the best he could every time.

"I have been successful probably because I have always realized that I knew nothing about writing and have merely tried to tell an interesting story entertainingly," he said. "But there is another reason (for success): From the beginning I have adhered to a policy of ordinary business honesty that was instilled in me by my father. My first stories were the best stories that I could write, and every story that I have written since has been the very best story that I could write. I have felt that it was a duty to those people who bought my books that I should give them the very best within me. I have no illusions as to the literary value of what I did give them, but I have the satisfaction of knowing that I gave them the best that my ability permitted."

You will be rejected in your career. Rejection is that fire that tempers a would-be writer into a professional. Writing itself never gets easier. After awhile, it simply *looks* easier, more relaxed, professional, as you discover the difference between a joist and a truss. But there will come a day as you learn your craft, as you learn what it takes to become a writer, to *be* a writer, that you will receive acceptance.

Exploring Anasazi ruins in the American Southwest.

# CHAPTER EIGHTEEN

Writing has changed dramatically within the past half-century, necessitating that writers adjust their craft to these changes, at least to some extent. Description and narrative summary occupied an important place in books, both fiction and nonfiction, up through the first half of the 20th Century. Movies and television made their debut, shortening attention spans as people grew accustomed to stories being told *only* in immediate scenes with as few interstices as possible. Rarely does a TV scene go past five seconds before cameras switch angles. Go much longer than that and you can almost hear a jaded and restless audience jumping on their remotes.

Theater devotees have likewise become impatient with narrative summary. Eugene O'Neil, Tennessee Williams, and Arthur Miller with their characters' long monologues began losing out to the snappy repertoire of Neil Simon.

Readers have followed the trend, responding to the "new" writing that consists as much as possible of immediate scenes with a minimum of transitional linkage. Henry James and James Jones yielded to Ernest Hemingway and Anna Quindlen. Zane Grey gave way to Louis L'Amour. Pace and suspense picked up to meet the shortened attention spans. Writers learned to jump-cut from one immediate scene to another, from one plot or subplot to the next.

When Zane Grey's *Wild Horse Mesa* was published in 1924, there was no television, most people attended movies infrequently and traveled long distances even less. Therefore, it was necessary that locales readers had never personally visited be described, as Grey did in this scene.

"The cloud above Wild Horse Mesa broke in the center and spread slowly, while the gray color almost imperceptibly changed. Between the mesa and the mountain slope sank a vast deep notch, through which V-shaped portal the ends of the earth seemed visible. Low down the distant rock surfaces were gold;

above them the belt of sky was yellowing. Canopying this band of pale sky stretched a roof of cloud, an extension of that canopy enshrouding the mesa, and it had begun to be affected by the sinking sun. At first the influence was gradual; then suddenly occurred swift changes, beautiful and evanescent—white clouds turning to rose, with centers of opal, like a coral shell."

Today, there is no longer a need for lengthy narrative description. All you have to do is see the word "Arizona" and an immediate picture forms in your mind because America is a traveling nation and those who haven't actually been to Arizona have seen it on television. Only 30 years later, when movies were popular and televisions were beginning to appear in every living room, L'Amour published *Kilkenny*. The trend toward more minimalist writing had already begun. Look at the difference between Grey's more static scene description and L'Amour's *Something* must always be happening.

"Riding on, he studied the valley. To right and left lay towering ridges that walled the valley in, and to the east other peaks lifted, and west the valley swung hard around and at one corner the wall was broken sharply off to fall sheer away for more than six hundred feet. Kilkenny paused long upon the lip, looking out over the immeasurable distance toward the faraway line of the purple hills. It was then that he first became conscious of the sound, a faint scarcely discernible whispering..."

Skip ahead once more to the year 2000 and *The Lawless Land* by Dusty Richards.

"Drago lay on his belly, overlooking a dry wash. He raised the new oily-smelling .44/.40 Winchester to his shoulder. Greasewood branches and tall dry grass rustled around him. A cresote odor hung in the hot air. He could look up and study the peaks of Mount Lemmon to his left. It would be much cooler up there. Hot sunshine glinted off the deep sand in the crossing and forced him to squint..."

Zane Grey used a long paragraph in which he described nothing but setting. L'Amour shortened description and melded it into narrative action. Richards completes the transition so that something is happening in virtually every sentence, and the sentences are short. "Dry wash" and "greasewood branches" and "peaks of Mount Lemmon" are not even described, but don't they evoke images nonetheless?

Riding horses 150 miles across Alaska.

This same phenomena has occurred throughout the business—from books and magazine articles to short stories and travelogues. Get to the point. Keep the action moving. William and Henry James with their longest sentences and paragraphs in English-language literature probably couldn't get a manuscript past an editor's transom today.

If you watch people browsing in book stores, you find they go to the section that interests them most—romance, men's adventure, science fiction, etc—and that the first thing they look at is the title cover. If that captures them, they look at the flaps or back cover narrative, after which, if they're still hooked, they open the book and skim the first page or two. Only if the book still commands their attention and imagination do they buy it. Otherwise, back to the shelf it goes, orphaned again.

This observation on how people buy books is a major lesson on how you should write books. You're not paying attention if "my novel really only gets started on page 20." Henry James and Henry Miller draw a yawn and a reject. Something exciting had better be happening quickly. Who can resist imaginative opening lines like, "The last camel died at noon?" (Ken Follett in *Key To Rebecca*). Or like, "I was trapped in a house with a lawyer, a barebreasted woman, and a dead man. The rattlesnake in the paper sack only complicated matters?" (Earl Emerson in *Fat Tuesday*).

In my books, fiction and nonfiction, I jump into the middle of action in the first chapter. I can always fill in the background later.

> There was no moon at the moment, but there would be one later. It would be red and menacing like the Japanese Rising Sun, and it would ride low on the watery horizon of the wartime Pacific, building a bloody shimmering boulevard across the sea to the two PT boats whose navy crew would await the outcome of the raid. Aboard the PT boats in the near-total pre-moon darkness, two teams of 6th Army Alamo Scouts—thirteen elite soldiers—prepared to slip over the PT gunnels into a pair of rubber boats...
> *Raider* (St. Martin's, 2002)

A writer should always keep in mind the relationship between the author, the book, and the book's intended audience. It's part of the craft of writing. The author creates the book, the intended purpose of which is to evoke emotion in the reader. That emotion is stimulated by the suspense of what will happen next. Readers need to know what it is the protagonist wants (the bone), what prevents him from getting it, and how he overcomes obstacles in striving to get it. The most profound suspense comes from a character with whom the reader identifies strongly and for whom he cares, who is torn by a difficult choice not yet made, and who is thrown into increasingly challenging circumstances. And today he wants all that in tightly-written scenes without a lot of description narrative.

Recognizing the constantly changing nature of the publishing business and the elements of what goes into a book or novel, magazine article or short story is a giant step toward learning craft and eventually reaching success.

### # # #

Another major change in publishing is the proliferation of genres in both books and magazines. My trusty Funk & Wagnells describes "genre" as a "particular category of art or literature characterized by a certain form, style or subject matter." No one is quite sure precisely when or where the term originated, but it was becoming common by the 1950s. The "Penny Westerns" back in the Old West was a genre, although it was not called that.

There were still a limited number of genres in the 1960s. These were broken down into a few major categories—western, romance, science fiction, suspense, action, and one or two others. Today, genres have blossomed into sub-genres and into sub-sub-genres. Romances, for example, have become Modern Western romances, Historical romances, Christian romances, etc. Science fiction claims perhaps 20 or more sub-genres. So do mysteries.

There's a snobbish tendency in the "literary" world to divide "mainstream" writing from "genre" writing. Mainstream writers often tend to look down upon genre writers as producing an inferior form of writing. Bluntly put, in the fewest possible words, that's a load of bull crap. Genre authors like W.E.B. Griffin and Stephen Coontz are every bit as skilled as John Irving; they also sell more books. *Gone With The Wind* would be considered a "romance" today. One of the most beautifully-written books I've ever read of any type is a romance, *Honey Moon* by Susan Elizabeth Phillips. The most brilliant, most imaginative writer I know is science fiction writer Tad Williams in his *Otherland* series.

I consider genres one of the best thing to come down the pike for both readers and writers. Genres provide readers with a wide variety of books to satisfy their reading tastes while at the same time opening more doors for writers. No matter the field or market, however, writing books and getting them published requires first-rate writing. Sloppiness in any genre equals failure.

Karen Joy Fowler (*Sarah Canary; Sister Noon*) writes both genre and mainstream. "On a good day I feel my work has benefited from the cross-pollination," she said, "and nothing matters as much as the quality of the work itself."

Much the same trend that busted novels into genres also splintered magazines. Your local 1930s drug store magazine rack could hold a copy of virtually every periodical released in the United States that month. It would take an entire store to hold all the magazines published today. The pulps and slicks from the 1950s—*Life* and *Look* and the others—have largely been replaced by hundreds if not thousands of special interest magazines directed toward specific slices of the market. Magazines cater to knitting, animal care, art and architecture, camping, sex, humor, history, ecology, religion, gays, paper flowers, quilts, dolls... If you're into donning black leather, tying up your partner and flogging him or her with a feather duster, there's a magazine for you. That's how focalized the market has become.

I made my living primarily by writing for magazines during the first five years or so of my full-time freelancing career. A goodly part of the so-called "big" magazines from which F. Scott Fitzgerald and Ernest Hemingway commanded huge sums were gone. However, by varying my interests, I found a paying market somewhere for literally any subject I wanted to write about. In those days, I wrote about a lot of different times and blanketed the world with my manuscripts to stave off the wolf at the door of the tool shed.

It turns out one of the most thrilling fishing spots on any water, fresh or salt, may soon disappear because there are *too* many fish and sports anglers insisting that spawning salmon *will* hit...

"Last Of The River King," *Great Lakes Fisherman*

The Apache wars in the Southwest ended when 57-year-old Geronimo and his band surrendered to General Nelson A. Miles in Arizona's Skeleton Canyon on September 5, 1886. Geronimo's breakout from the San Carlos Apache reservation had left fourteen Americans dead in the United States and between 500 and 600 Mexicans dead south of the border. Geronimo lost only two braves...

"'Civilizing' Geronimo," *True West*

# # #

A third major trend that should greatly concern writers and the writing craft is so insidious, so intellectually insulting, and so dangerous to freedom of speech and the press that it should be addressed rather at length. The "political correctness" movement, which asserts that none of us should offend in any way any other group either intentionally or inadvertently, is systematically mugging writers of our language and the depths of understanding to which unfettered language is capable of reaching.

Formerly, it was a writer's calling, his duty, to jolt, cajole, to offend, to satire, to drive language and thought into different realms of truth and meaning. Not anymore. Today, truth should be suppressed or softened or diluted or ignored if it offends. *Huck Finn* is only one of many books being driven underground because they are decreed offensive to one group or another. Writers are being herded into a conformity of thought and expression whose greatest ambition is not to offend.

Such is the climate in modern America that I wrote *Liberty City* (AmErica House, 2000), re-read it, and suffered an overwhelming compulsion to apologize for it. Like I had been caught having sex with a farm animal, only incomparably worse. Sodomy with a cow or a sheep could be understood and forgiven, providing I apologized to the animal, sought counseling and joined a support group. What would be less readily understood and forgiven in an age of acute sensitivity was my daring to venture into unpopular thought, to offer myself as a critic for prevailing social ideology. Soberly, almost guiltily, I realized I would be accused of being afflicted with every modern "ism" imaginable—racism, sexism, homophobia-ism, specie-ism. You name it. I would be charged with *hating*. I felt I should run through the streets begging forgiveness from every stranger I met. *Look at me! I don't hate anybody!*

Needless to say, I couldn't find a major publication for it. I finally published through a publish on demand house because I thought it should be out there.

> "Let us pray," said the Reverend, bowing his head and clasping his hands. "...Grace, mercy, peace and justice will be with us from God the Father-Mother and from Jesus Christ, Child of the Father-Mother—"
>
> Thomas Wright lifted his head slightly and opened one eye to peer past Kelli to where Jamison sat next to them with his wife Rachael. Jamison's one eye looked back at him. They nodded at each other. Then they got up and walked out of church together.
>
> Kelli refused to speak to her husband on the way home. As soon as he parked the station wagon in their drive, she burst into tears and jumped out, exclaiming, "You embarrassed me, walking out like that!"
>
> "I want God to be a man," Thomas said. "I want Him strong and fierce. I want Him to smite sinners and cast demons into hell. I don't want a faggy Jesus and a bisexual God undergoing therapy."
>
> *Liberty City* (AmErica House, 2000)

I tried satire again with *Going Bonkers: The Wacky World of Cultural Madness*, a nonfiction book, the premise being that if individuals can go wacky, eating bugs off the sidewalk, talking to sofas and sipping urine, is it not possible for an entire culture to go mad in the same way? An editor of a major publishing house with whom I had published a dozen previous books immediately took umbrage at my proposal. I was "reactionary." What may seem wacky to some, she said, is perfectly reasonable to others.

I wrote back asking if it were wacky or reasonable for a professor of drama to be sacked for teaching the classic theater of Shakespeare, Aeschylus and Ibsen because "feminists are offended by the selection of works from a sexist European canon?" That instead of *Othello* or *The Cherry Orchard*, the theater department should approve the production of *Betty The Yeti*, about a logger who becomes an environmentalist after having sex with a lady Sasquatch in the Pacific Northwest?

Was it wacky or reasonable, I submitted, for feminists to insist that men should sit or squat to urinate because for them to stand at the function, which women cannot, is "overtly macho" and therefore offensive?

Was it wacky or reasonable that children at one school should be denied the opportunity to see the ballet *Romeo And Juliet* because their school felt it to be a "blatantly heterosexual love story?"

George Orwell in his social novel *1984* created a "Newspeak" vocabulary to provide an approved medium of expression for a *proper* political viewpoint. Expressions of unorthodox opinions were to be rendered obsolete in two ways: first, by eliminating undesirable words, changing their meanings or stripping them of old unorthodox meanings; second, by deliberately constructing new words intended to impose a desirable political attitude upon people using them. Reality and truth were whatever the Party held to be real and true. Truth was flexible, mobile, ever-changing. Viewpoints and opinions were switched as readily as changing socks.

Consider these sensitive and politically correct times when we are losing word after word from our language while at the same time the meanings of other words are being obfuscated or transformed into a meaningless psycho-babble of lukewarm pabulum. The modern approach to language and the facts language symbolize is to make them conform socially and politically. Call it the blanding of America. A highly cultivated ignorance in ignoring the obvious. A growing verbal anesthesia. Empty, inoffensive, bloodless euphemisms are invented to replace simply descriptive terms: *differently abled, mentally challenged, significant other, undocumented alien...* Censoring words, changing and mushing their meanings, is also to censor thought, attitude, behavior. One school has declared the word "fairy" to be improper and has decreed that heretofore "elf" should be used instead. Tooth fairy is now the tooth elf.

Words control thought. Thought controls civilization. He who controls words controls thought controls civilization. Fueled by virtually every ethnic, religious and special interest group imaginable, people are being conditioned to suppress individual thought and spray forth *approved* opinions as automatically as a machine gun sprays bullets. Writers in this cautious cultural climate are pressed to guard their pens at all times out of fear of saying something that someone else might find offensive. George Orwell called it *Groupthink.*

A few years ago I published a nonfiction book about the Vietnam War. My editor telephoned me to suggest we delete from the manuscript all references to the enemy being called "gooks" or other derogatory terms.

"It's offensive to Vietnamese-Americans," he reasoned.

"No!" I responded. "That was part of the language of the time. Language is a part of history."

"But it is offensive these days."

I dug in. "We must not rewrite history. It is dangerous to rewrite the past in order to make it conform to the political expectations of today. If we start doing that, history is lost. It becomes whatever we want it to be to satisfy a particular political or social climate."

I was just as intransient when I received copyeditor notes back for *Detachment Delta: Operation Iron Weed* (Avon, 2003), the second of my War on Terror novel series. The copyeditor, whose only job is to correct grammar and structure and check facts, became offended, insulted, and took umbrage throughout the manuscript.

One of my characters, Mad Dog, is indeed obnoxious and uncouth. As an example of the copyeditor's intrusiveness and sensitivity, he wanted to change a quote by Mad Dog because it was "grotesque." The quote he wanted to change was, "Someone slapped you, you turned and knocked his dick in the dirt." What he wanted this rough Special Operations soldier to say was something like, "If you hit me, now, I'll hit you back." Give me a break.

My heroine is Jewish, and there is a repertoire between her and my hero when he thinks she is a male. He calls her a "Jew boy." The copyeditor found that "offensive" and wanted to cut it out.

"Too much," he scolded me when one of my black characters and a white character, close friends, are rapping on each other about race.

"Gratuitous, author insults immigrant types," he remarks at another point in which my characters are involved in Afghanistan fighting the Taliban.

"I hesitate to cut dialogue for being offensive (although I have in a few places in this manuscript). Here, this opening paragraph is *so offensive* and *ugly* that I *suggest* (emphasis his) cutting all four paragraphs." Mad Dog again. He hated Mad Dog.

"Overdone and parts are gratuitously offensive... Bigoted and nasty," he commented about Mad Dog's remark of "Dear God, save us from the assholes who believe in You."

Here are excerpts from the letter I fired back in protest:

"I think he (the copyeditor) did a splendid job when he stuck to copyediting. However, when he came to much of the other, stepped to far into PC, he became a total idiot. I intended to let it pass, but when his comments became personally insulting, as though I and not my characters were personally offending his obviously-heightened sensitivities, then I decided I would have to make my own comments.

"Please forgive me for responding harshly in some of the page-by-page comments below to his notes, but after awhile when his comments became accusatory and frustrating, when he stopped judging my work and my characters and began to self-righteously and smugly judge me personally, I had had enough.

"Point being, I know these men I write about personally. They're rough, they're tough, and some twerp comes around high-hatting them, condescending to them, they will, in spite of the copyeditor's objection to the crude language, 'knock his dick in the dirt.'

"In my military stories, I intend to write gritty, realistic stories about real men. SpecOps types could care less about political correctness. They are what they are, and I would—and have many times—trusted my life to them. When I go to war, I want to go with men like those in DELTA—Mad Dog Carson, Thumbs Jones, Brandon Kragle, the General—not a bunch of COO (consideration of others) feminized eunuchs who will get my ass waxed. I know the language of these men, the rough way they talk, the insults and bantering—and, yes, the courage, the love they have for one another, the respect, the patriotism. These are the kind of men I write about, in their own language.

"A writer should write true, to reflect his slice of life the way it really is, not the way some twerp would have it be, even if we all are forced to attend Sensitivity Training. If he thinks I'm objectionable, he should talk to Cdr. Roy Boehm, my friend and the man who organized and trained the first Navy SEALs, or my other friend, Command Sergeant Major Galen Kittleson, former Alamo Scout, Green Beret, and the only American in history to make four raids to free POWs in two wars, or Richard Marcinko of SEAL Team Six. He should hear what *they* would have to say should he infer they were bigoted and offensive..."

The editor, Michael Shohl, is a friend and a man of common sense. He agreed with me. In spite of the copyeditor's attempt to censor me, the book was published as I intended it to be, language and all. Such censorship has become so common in the publishing business that many houses won't publish anything that seems offensive politically or socially.

In this strange new world, honest thinking men are unable to disagree without the one branding the other in order to shut him up. Such methods have rendered many topics taboo to discussion. Disagree with affirmative action? Here comes the wrath of the *racism* label. Question the idea of women in combat? Watch out. *Sexism* will blow your hat off just above the shoulders. Criticize the mayor of New York for marching in a Gay Pride parade with near-naked men simulating homosexual sex? You must be a *homophobe*. Ridicule Hollywood celebrities for standing naked in the snow to protest wearing furs? That's *specie-ism*. It goes on and on.

Increasingly, editors give the materials they receive the "sensitivity test" before accepting for publication.

Admittedly, I grew up in the hills of a part-Indian hillbilly clan of migrant farm workers. We were an ignorant, backward bunch. But what we hillbillies possessed instead of sophistication was a fiercely independent nature and a rough-spoken language which expressed our world viewpoint directly, clearly, and left no doubt as to meaning. If a man thought you were an idiot, he called you an idiot and to hell with your self-esteem.

Should we writers now feel guilty and relinquish an honest truthful approach to writing because some people, being frail and cowardly creatures, seek to escape the freedom of different ideas? Should we cower before the Contemporary Commandment that, first, above all else, thou shalt not offend and, in never offending, further diminish our range of thought? Should we remain passive and mute while allowing ourselves to perform the essential Jonah act of being swallowed by a monster without at least protesting in the best way we know how—through the free, unfettered use of words and language?

Not on your life. Let other writers more timid run through the streets and apologize for what we should be. I, for one, will continue to seek truth in my writing. If it offends, so be it.

Skiing in Colorado

# CHAPTER NINETEEN

"Our trip to Disney World was an unforgettable experience. We all got up early and had breakfast, then we packed the car and left, full of anticipation. The day was fine and we had fun on the way. When we had bought our tickets, we rode the monorail craning our necks to see the wonderful sights. It was one of the most thrilling experiences I've ever had. We took a boat trip down a jungle river and saw many interesting animals. It was just like Africa. Then we visited a western frontier town, which gave us valuable knowledge about American history..."

Have I lost you yet? In this brief passage I have either failed to use or have misused virtually every tool in the writer's craft box, with the possible exception that I wrote in short sentences. This kind of writing would never sustain a full magazine article, much less a book. But even were it completed, it has about as much chance of being published as a sigh does of surviving a whirlwind.

A friend of mine, editor of a major publishing house, explained the practical way in which books are selected for publication. The process begins with the company's purchasing board designating a set number of books and their genres that will be purchased during the year. Each editor is then assigned responsibility for finding, buying (with the approval of the board) and editing his share of this number. Perhaps 20,000 manuscripts or more will tumble across his desk, out of which he will select three, four, six, whatever, but a relatively small number.

Obviously, he will select the best and most marketable. Even with such an enormous "slush pile" from which to make his decision, however, the deadline may catch him. He may then be forced to hurriedly pick a manuscript in order to beat the deadline. That is how second-rate and even bad books sometimes get published.

Do you want to be one of those who continues to write bad books and hopes lightning will strike when some editor's deadline catches him? Or, do you want to learn your craft—how to drive a nail, pour concrete, miter a joint—so that your manuscript comes into major consideration and eventual publication?

"Some people are born word deaf the way some people are born tone deaf to music," said Charles Champlin, then-editor of the Los Angeles *Times*. "But I think anyone who has any sensitivity to words can be helped to write better, to get over some of the hurdles, to avoid some of the traps that other people have got into before them."

Most of what I've learned about writing, I've learned the hard way. By *doing*. As there are hundreds, even thousands, of good books on what I call the "nuts and bolts" of writing, I won't attempt to mire myself inside the engine of our craft to explain how it works. Rather, I want to concentrate on general concepts and principals of *what* a successful writer should know when it comes to craft.

# # #

"There are three rules for writing fiction," Somerset Maugham once commented. "Unfortunately, no one can agree on what they are."

Perhaps. But there is at least one general rule on writing upon which all writers agree. It is that the most important element of all is *story*. With the advent of the so-called nonfiction book—a true story told using the techniques of fiction—both fiction and nonfiction require near-identical considerations. People read for entertainment or to learn something, often both. Either way, they want to know what happens next. The more skillfully we use the tools of our craft to build suspense, to unfold the story in a constant state of tension until the climax, the more successful we are bound to be in our careers.

Selecting and planning the story is the first step in the process of writing a book. Story entails conflict. Conflict means characters involved in action with a beginning, a middle, and an end in which the conflict is resolved. Therefore, the first question that should be asked about any potential project is: Does the story have enough substance to support a book-length work, or would it be better told in a shorter medium?

As I have authored several nonfiction books with historical figures (*First SEAL* with Roy Boehm; *The Walking Dead* with Craig Roberts; *Hill 488* with Ray Hildreth; *Taking Fire* with Ron Alexander; *Doc: Platoon Medic* with Daniel E. Evans), I often receive queries from people who want me to write books with them about their experiences. I turn most of them down because their stories encompass a single event in which the prospective co-author plays a relatively minor role. There simply isn't enough upon which to focus a full-length manuscript.

*Taking Fire* was a noted exception. The story met all the criteria of substance and conflict—flying helicopters in Vietnam during the war. Readers would identify with the universal element of a brave individual coping with combat. It touched the reader's emotion. The motivation behind the story was fresh and original, the plot new and exciting. It was the kind of story I liked to read—and therefore to write.

Lieutenant Ron Alexander endured 13 months of sustained combat in Vietnam without once being struck by enemy fire. Although he was under five-feet-four in stature, which made him ineligible to fly helicopters because of a height restriction, he still wriggled his way into the air to become a near-legend in the 1st Air Cavalry as "Mini-Man," his call sign. The other pilots labeled him "charmed" as again and again he flew into the middle of action to rescue downed airmen, LRRPs, and soldiers penned down by the enemy.

> Sweat rolled from underneath my helmet and streamed down my face. I sweated all the way to my crotch. I couldn't tell if it was sweat or if I had pissed my pants. My bone joints felt fused together. Whereas most pilots flew with their heels braced against the floor, I was too short. I had to fly with my

legs stuck straight out. Same for my arms, which were likewise too short. It had always been a handicap not to be able to steady my elbows on my thighs. Other pilots ribbed me about looking like a little kid trying to reach the pedals to drive his dad's Chevy. Lieutenant Ron Alexander, call sign *Mini-Man*. Shortest helicopter pilot in Vietnam and the U.S. Army. A quarter-inch *shorter* than regs allowed...

Tracer bullets were much brighter at night. Especially when they came close. Greenish-white balls of fire, each appearing about the size of a basketball, rushed up out of the darkness of the forest and past the helicopter like a string of UFOs in a hurry...

*Taking Fire* (with Ron Alexander, St. Martin's, 2001)

How well did it make the grade for story content?

"A rousing tale, full of sharp details and told in the hard language of soldiers baptized in fire."—*Kirkus Review.*

"An honest and exciting narrative of the stress of war."—*Library Journal.*

"Whether he's flying combat missions, lying in his bunk, or drinking beer with his crew, our hero is quick to offer his opinions on the war and share his emotions with the reader. This is, without a doubt, an honest and sincere account of a chopper pilot's tour of duty in Vietnam."—*The Roanoke Times.*

# # #

You must now consider the practical approach to writing the book after selecting the story and planning its general content. Will it be told in first person or third person, rarely in second person? I wrote my novel *The 100th Kill* from a journalist's first person point of view while telling the sniper's story from third person POV. It was an experiment that worked.

Structure is important. Structure is vital. That means *plotting*. Plotting a novel and plotting a nonfiction book require similar considerations. The major difference is that the plot for the nonfiction book is already laid out for you; you simply have to determine the best way to tell the story.

"There are nine-and-sixty ways of constructing tribal lays," Rudyard Kipling wrote, advice that can well be applied to plotting, "and every single one of them is right."

James Michener plotted the details of every scene and chapter in his novels before he ever began writing. I do just the opposite. In a novel, I know the beginning, I know the major characters, and I know the general ending. What happens between the two points is anybody's guess. What works for one writer when it comes to plotting may not work for another.

Plot, like scenes within a plot, involves three factors—a situation, a complication, and a resolution of that complication. Always think conflict. Two dogs fighting over a bone with the outcome always in doubt until the end. The storyline progresses in a series of catastrophes, reversals and breakthroughs. What I call "one damned thing after the other." Every time the hero gains an inch here, he loses an inch there. Tension is gradually built toward a climax, a denouement.

I have a friend who wants to be a writer, but she is so sweet-tempered that she absolutely cannot bear the thought of anything bad happening to her characters. As a result, even though she writes competently, everything comes up roses on every page, in every chapter. Never any conflict, never any suspense. She has yet to sell anything major.

I use the "River Model" to explain a dramatic book's structure. Rain is falling on the plains at the beginning of the story as the characters and setting are introduced and the conflict begins. This doesn't mean ten pages of narrative and exposition. Get into the story, but the rain is falling rather gently compared to the raging river it will eventually become.

> The bishop and other church staff were removing sleepy children from the orphanage and herding them across the darkened church yard toward a basement beneath the rectory. A young woman looked up as she hurried past with her

charges. Brandon recognized her from the morning. She was a tiny, well-built girl of about twenty-five or so with long sun-burnt hair and, he remembered, bright emerald eyes. He towered over her by at least a foot.

"I know you," he said.

"Yeah? We're going to have to stop meeting this way, Major." She kept going, disappearing in the night with the children.

*Detachment Delta: Operation Iron Weed* (Avon, 2003)

Suspense and conflict begins to build in the same way that rain gathers into runoff and runoff becomes streams racing toward the river.

Major Brandon Kragle looked around with pride at the determined, confident expressions on the hairy faces of his men. These were tough, intelligent soldiers who would literally go anywhere, anytime, to do any damned thing. Exactly as Colonel Charlie Beckwith and then Major Darren E. Kragle had intended when they built the elite counterterrorist force.

The General had the last word.

"It's an extremely hazardous assignment," he acknowledged, looking directly at his son. "It's a whole lot like a snail crawling across the edge of a razor blade. He can make it okay as long as he doesn't make a mistake and slip."

*Detachment Delta: Operation Iron Weed* (Avon, 2003)

The streams of the various internal and external plots and sub-plots flow into the river. The river rages with conflict and suspense. You know, you just *know*, there is a waterfall ahead.

As the men began digging in behind the boulders, scraping and mining with rifle butts, knives, or, like gophers, with their bare hands, Brandon crawled on his belly along the base of the cliff. It rose so sheer above him that even a tree toad with its suction-cup toes would have taken a second look. Escape downhill was out of the question. It was too exposed. Uphill appeared to be the only hope.

*Detachment Delta: Operation Iron Weed* (Iron Weed, 2003)

Rain falls on the plains and gathers in streams, streams rush into the raging river, the raging river roars toward the big climatic waterfall.

Slinging his submachine gun to free his other hand, Brandon felt his way along the wall at a trot, dragging Summer with him. Firing ceased except for an isolated jittery round. Men shouted orders and questions and ran blindly about. It seemed everyone in the cave, a collection of voices, all started talking and yelling at once. Good. It covered their escape...
*Detachment Delta: Operation Iron Weed* (Avon, 2003)

The waterfall takes the heroes over in a dramatic climax. Below, the giant pool allows the reader to come down from the high of having ridden the cataract.

They came out of the trees on the pathway as a Yellow cab from Memphis negotiated its way up the long drive to the main house. It stopped and a small figure got out. It was clad head to toe in a black Afghan burqa. A veil covered the face, except for the eyes, which were an incredible emerald as Summer looked up and saw Brandon running toward her, laughing.
*Detachment Delta: Operation Iron Weed* (Avon, 2003)

# # #

There is a strong relationship between story, plot, and *characterization*. Each supports and feeds upon the others. Always think of characterization and how best to reveal it within the plot. It is revealed through description, action, dialogue, internal thoughts, gestures and mannerisms, opinions of other characters, the setting of the book, the character's tastes and interests, contradictions and consistencies...

Walter Cronkite, "the most trusted man in America," was now talking about the war every night on the news. Friends asked me if I weren't afraid of going. Nah. There were already enough Marines in Vietnam to handle the job without adding me to the number. I could wear the good-looking uniform and have the name without the game. Besides, when you were a strapping eighteen-year-old kid a couple of inches under six feet tall and full of yourself, you thought you were going to live forever...

*Hill 488* (with Ray Hildreth, Pocket Books, 2003)

Since dialogue is essential to both characterization and to the plot and movement of the story, and since dialogue is the most difficult part of writing for many writers, I would like to pass on several basic rules of dialogue that I have learned over the years. Dialogue must sound "real" while at the same time it can only be an approximation, a condensation of the way people talk. I often critique novels and books in which the dialogue rambles on and on, complete with "As you know, Joe" and "Uh" and "How do you do? I'm fine, how are you?" This may, in fact, be the way people *really* talk, but ordinary conversation when read is *boring.*

The first rule is that dialogue should be brief. If it should necessarily run into a monologue, convince the reader that it is important, then break it into brief segments with narrative interruptions. More than three or four sentences in a speech runs into danger.

Second: Dialogue should never be used simply for its own sake. It should add to reader's knowledge of story and character or not used at all. It should keep the story focused and moving forward.

Third: Eliminate all the routine exchanges of ordinary conversation, the "how's the wife and children" parts. What you want to do is convey a sense of spontaneity while avoiding the repetitiveness of true conversation.

Fourth: Use dialogue to reveal the speaker's character, both directly and indirectly, through his manner of speech, use of language, speech tags and focus.

Finally: Dialogue should allow the reader to read between the lines, to understand the conversation as much through stage direction, actions and gestures as in what is actually spoken.

> Two men were holding hands. One man was crying. A short man had his pack strapped to a bicycle, and a taller one had two live ducks in a ruck. A third clutched a squawking chicken.
>
> Stunned, I turned to Nguyen Hai.
>
> "They to eat," was the automatic response. Even Sergeant Nguyen—*he* did not want to go.
>
> "How in hell can we go on patrol sounding like a poultry farm?" I demanded.
>
> "No sweat," Hai said matter-of-factly. "VC alla time know we come anyhow."
>
> I began to sputter, made speechless by the marked contrast between the raggedy-ass bunch before me now and the Marines back in Mike Company—weary and disease-ridden as those Marines might be. I found my voice and began to shout at the patrol, spitting droplets and shaking my fist. The chicken squawked louder.
>
> I paused to catch my breath and let Nguyen translate. The sergeant barked a few words, condensing the English, and then looked toward me to continue.
>
> "You weren't translating word for word," I accused. "What did you tell them?" "I tell them you will kill them," Nguyen said innocently, adding casually after a pause, "Them believe you."
>
> *The Walking Dead* (with Craig Roberts, Pocket Books, 1989)

The other techniques of writing—flashbacks, plants, foreshadowing, pacing, action and narrative, scene and sequel, selection of detail, knowing what to leave in and what to take out—are your hammers and nails, saws, planes and adzes in the process of constructing conflict, creating characters and building suspense. They help you to build bones and flesh and blood into your story. Learn what they are and how to use them. Without them, your story reverts to little more than "Our trip to Disney World..."

I foreshadowed, for example, on the very first page, first scene of *The 100th Kill* to give the reader a subconscious glimpse of the climatic conflict between my sniper and my journalist. See if you can pick out the germane passage.

The kid's face frame the first time in the Nikon's range-finder. It was like the 135mm lens magnified and brought out something not readily apparent to the naked eye.

I dropped the lens from my eye.

He became just another kid of thousands swept across the Big Pond since LBJ started his buildup by landing Marines at China Beach. Maybe his face was even a little more boyish than most. I doubt if he had even shaved before he enlisted in the Marines Corps, the Crotch, the by-God U.S. Marines. He was blond and high 'n tight on the sides so that his head looked almost bald around the pulled-low patrol cap.

I swept off my boonie hat and wiped the Vietnam sweat out of my eyes and off my face.

The kid remained perfectly motionless. He lay prone behind a log, posing for the camera, the sling of the 30.06 Winchester Model 70 snugly around his forward arm to steady the 8x sniperscope through which, unblinking, he peered directly at me. It seemed a natural position for him...

The rifle made me nervous.

"That goddamned thing *is* unloaded?" I asked him.

"Of course, sir. I would never point a loaded weapon at someone I didn't intend to kill, sir. Would you?"

*The 100th Kill* (Pocket Books, 1992)

You're right if you picked out the last quote.

# # #

"When you write, try to leave out all the parts readers skip," advised Elmore Leonard. Make every word count, do the necessary rewrites, then end it.

Knowing when and how to end a book is just as important as knowing when and how to begin it. Actor Kevin Spacey tells the story of how his father wanted to write the Great American Novel. He worked most of his life on it.

"Someday," he kept saying, "I'm going to get it published, but it's not good enough yet."

Kevin found the manuscript after his father died, still being rewritten.

At a recent writers conference, I met a man who sought my advice on what to do with a science fiction novel he had been writing and rewriting for the past five years. I thought of Kevin Spacey's father.

"Do one of three things with it," I told him. "Stuff it back in a drawer, toss it out, or finish it now and get on to something else."

Far too many novice writers seem to take to heart Truman Capote's remark that "finishing a book is just like you took a child out in the back yard and shot it." They don't want to do that. I suspect, however, that more times than not the reluctance to finish a book is because the author is afraid to toss it out to editors and face possible rejection.

It has to be shot sometime if you're going to be a writer. Finish it, shoot it out there, then get on to something else.

There are any number of ways to end a book in a way that will let the characters go on living in the reader's mind long after he finishes the last page—and make him want to read your next book. The conclusion does not have to be happy, but it must be satisfying. It must end because that is the way it *has* to end. How else could *Gone With The Wind* have climaxed other than Scarlett's looking toward a new day?

Who can forget the final scene in *For Whom The Bell Tolls* when Robert Jordan, wounded, is left behind when the guerrilla band flees ahead of the enemy's approach? In a heartbreaking encounter, he forces Maria to get on her horse and go with the others. Then he lies on the ground and waits...

"He was waiting until the officer reached the sunlit place where the first trees of the pine forest joined the green slope of the meadow. He could feel his heart beating against the pine needle floor of the forest." The End

A book ends soon after the point of recognition or soon after the close of the struggle and the ownership of the bone is ascertained. It must end dramatically—the waterfall—then quickly smooth out into the peaceful pool to let the reader settle down into acceptance and understanding.

> "Cameron, there's something else I wanted you to know," the Major ventured. "Gypsy wasn't dead when we landed in Turkmenistan. She wanted me to tell you something. She wanted me to tell you that she loved you."
>
> It was a lie. Cameron knew it was a lie, but he also knew telling it was a painful sacrifice for his brother, who also loved the brave little redhead from Funny Platoon. The gesture brought tears to Cameron's eyes. Unable to speak, he simply turned and embraced his older brother.
>
> To everyone's surprise, the General turned and hugged Cassidy. Then he stepped around the grave and hugged each of his other sons. He regained his composure, looked around to make sure no one had seen, straightened his uniform, and marched out of the cemetery at the head of the Kragle clan of warriors.
>
> *Detachment Delta: Punitive Strike* (Avon, 2002)

# # #

Over the years, from my own writing and from teaching and critiquing other writers, I have discovered beginning writers unsure of their craft consistently make the same mistakes. I have isolated the ten most common of these and now list them in order of importance:

One—Overwriting, or what I call expository diarrhea or "step-by-step" writing, in which a character's every action is so faithfully recorded that it is as though he were being videotaped.

Two—Poor dialogue written too "realistically" and without focus.

Three—Obscure writing, hard to understand because you fail to say exactly what you mean.

Four—Anti-climatic sentences and paragraphs. Place the most important part at the end of the sentence or the paragraph. "John died on Thursday after the rattlesnake bit him." Huh-uh. Make it read, "The rattlesnake bit John, and he died on Thursday." John's dying is the most important part of the sentence.

Five—Misdirected antecedents. "Feeling disheartened, the hospital called John on Thursday. The *hospital* feels disheartened?

Six—Poor leads that do not grab. Think of such reader grabbers as: "Lee was in the ladies room when the bomb went off." (*Dutch Shea Jr.,* by John Gregory Dunne); or "Some women give birth to murderers, some go to bed with them, and some marry them." *(Before The Fact,* by Francis Iles).

Seven—Abruptly changing focus, as from one character or scene to the next.

Eight—Soapboxing. "Think pieces" in which the writer lectures the reader rather than sticking to facts and the story.

Nine—Misspellings and grammatical mistakes in the submitted manuscript.

Ten—Failure to rewrite—of, conversely, too many rewritings in which the heart of the story is simply stabbed to death and loses its life.

# CHAPTER TWENTY

The triad of *Research*, Marketing and Promotion are the most overlooked and undervalued skills of the writer's craft. That's especially true of Marketing and Promotion.

"Good writing," admonished *Writer's Market 2003*, "is useless if you don't know which markets will buy your work or how to pitch and sell your writing."

For me, Research is the most enjoyable of the triad. Getting the facts, and getting the facts right, are essential to the credibility of your work and to your own personal integrity. That's as true in fiction as in nonfiction. If you make a mistake or get something wrong in a book, some reader will catch it and let you know.

In my first *Delta* series novel, *Detachment Delta: Punitive Strike*, I had F-16 fighter jets being launched from the U.S. nuclear aircraft carrier *Abraham Lincoln*. I knew better; I was merely careless. F-16s are Air Force planes; F-14s and F-18s are navy planes used on carriers. After all, I had just spent a week sailing on the *Abe Lincoln* from San Diego to Seattle with my sailor son Joshua. An alert reader, as humor columnist Dave Barry would put it, caught the SNAFU and let me know right away.

While we are admonished to write what we know, we can still know many things. For a freelancer, becoming an "expert" on an assortment of topics means the difference between writing ad nauseum on a single topic and writing on a variety of subjects for many different publishers. It also makes a big difference in income. In my long career, I have written on issues ranging from how to change a baby's diapers to how to garrote an enemy.

The editor of *Popular Science* telephoned to ask if I could do a 1,000-word piece on the most "realistic" combat video games. I had never played a video game in my life, but that didn't mean I couldn't become an "expert." Which I did. In short order. For which I received a check for $700.

My personal research methods include interviews with experts, library research, and, of course, since I consider myself a "participatory journalist," trips into the field to gain experience first hand. Generally, I utilize all three methods.

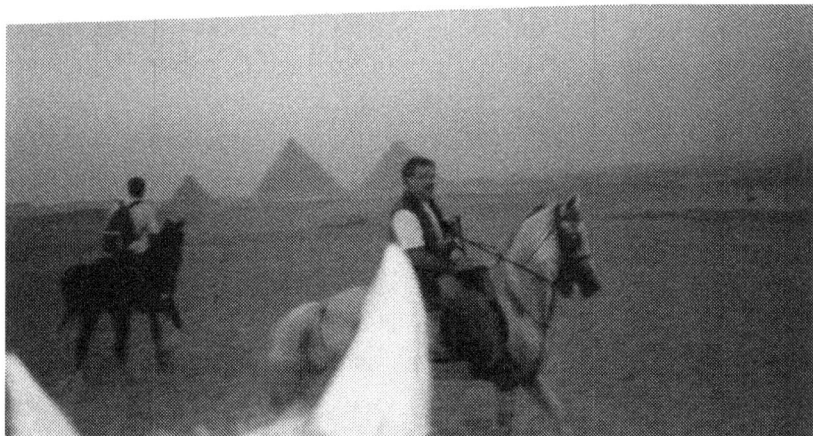

Riding in Egypt, with the Great Pyramids in the background.

For example, I interviewed more than 100 people for *Smoke Jumpers*. I read a dozen different books on subjects such as fire-fighting techniques and firefighter training, on how forests grew, on the mechanics of fire, and on aircraft and firefighting histories. I went through newspaper and magazine articles for information on the nation's most disastrous fires and the destruction and fatalities they caused. Then I visited a smokejumper training camp, made a parachute jump with a team, and drove to Colorado to take a close look at Storm King Mountain, where fourteen brave jumpers and "hot shots" died in a blow-up.

I had to be dragged screaming into the age of cyberspace. Once I got there, however, I found the information-rich internet to be a motherlode for the researcher. I now use it extensively, along with my "clip files" of newspaper and newspaper articles. One thing though with the internet—you have to be careful to separate the wheat from the chaff. And there's a lot of chaff.

*The Encyclopedia of Navy SEALs* (Facts On File, 2002), with its more than 2,000 entries, was the most extensive-research book I have ever written. I spent months interviewing and gathering materials before I ever began writing. Books, clip files, internet copies, photographs, documents, lists of contacts, audio and video tapes, and other data piled up knee-deep in my office. It was a daunting task, one I'm not inclined to repeat in the near future.

Nothing, however, ever seems to go to waste. Each project generates a ton of notes, recordings, book, photographs, and other materials that, sooner or later, provides a source for other books and magazine articles.

In 1994, I was the first civilian journalist to be granted full access to participate in operations with the United States Coast Guard. My military background helped open the doors. For a month I sailed with the USCG cutter *Padre* out of Key West, Florida, intercepting drug smugglers, rescuing Cuban refugees from the Straits, and patrolling the Caribbean. I flew Falcon interceptor jets using FLIR (forward looking infrared radar) to seek out drug boats and participated in small boat and helicopter rescue operations.

Although I intended to write a book, the project fell through for a variety of reasons. Nonetheless, the data I gathered did not go to waste. I wrote a number of magazine articles.

The Coast Guard, especially the "Coasties" of the 7th Division in Florida, has been fighting this peacetime war against an army of smugglers for over a decade, from the jungle rivers of Colombia and Panama to the Caribbean Gulf Stream to the skies over Jamaica and Cuba.

"You get out there, it doesn't take you long to realize this is a real shooting war," declared Coast Guard Boatswain's Mate R.C. Ladnier...

"Special Operations Against 'Caribbean Snow,'" *Behind The Lines*

I used my acquired knowledge of the Coast Guard in my *Delta* novel series about the War on Terror.

> Restless, Thornton climbed to the flying bridge of the USCG *Padre* to get a little fresh salt air while he scanned the blue horizon in the direction of Cuba, not really expecting to see anything yet. Just watching and trying not to think of his stomach. He wore a blue uniform *Padre* ball cap to protect his shaved head from the tropical sun. Even men as black as he were susceptible to sunburn...
> *Detachment Delta: Operation Deep Steel* (Avon, 2004)

Let me point out, again, that perfectly competent books are published every year through less-extensive research efforts than the ones I employ. For me, however, "participatory journalism" means I have to go and see and do for myself in order to fully understand and appreciate my subject and to write about it. Besides, going places, meeting new and exciting people, and having adventures are part of the fun of being a writer.

Even as I write this on a deadline, I am preparing to travel to Algeria to provide logistics and security support for a group of Christian missionaries delivering aid to refugee camps. Nancy Huff, the charming head of Teach The Children Inc., heard me speak at an Oklahoma State University writers conference and asked me to make the journey. Undoubtedly, the experience will end up in new books and articles.

It's all part of the "living many lives" dream I confided in my mom when I was seven-years-old.

### # # #

Marketing for the cutting-edge freelancer entails keeping up with what is selling at this particular moment while at the same time looking at trends in order to determine what will sell next month, next year. For me, magazine racks and book stores are like magnets. I cannot pass one without stopping to take a look. What subject matters are selling, what's hot now, what will be the rage six months from now, a year? Without the developed ability to market your product—and writers *do* produce a product—you will lose income to the point that you eventually have to retreat to a *real* job.

In 1989, my friend and partner Craig Roberts and I detected a trend toward a public interest in snipers. We published *One Shot-One Kill*, which literally opened the door for scores of sniper books that still stock book shelves. *One Shot* currently has nearly a quarter-million copies in print, has appeared in a number of different languages, and is found references in nearly every subsequent book about sniping.

> If you look at just the statistics, it is damned hard to kill an enemy soldier on the battlefield. During World War II, the Allies fired an average of 25,000 bullets for each enemy soldier they killed. The ratio of bullets to KIAs kept climbing. United Nations troops in Korea expended 50,000 rounds for each dead enemy. In Vietnam, American GI's armed with M-14s at the beginning of the war and, later, with rapid-firing M-16s burned up in excess of 200,000 bullets to get a single body count...
>
> *One Shot-One Kill* (with Craig Roberts, Pocket Books, 1990)

The book is still selling $13,000-$16,000 a year. Craig and I have just been signed by Pocket Books to write a sequel, bringing the story of sniping up to date with snipers in Panama, Bosnia, Afghanistan, Iraq and the War on Terror.

Because of my constant research and marketing, I predicted the War on Terror years before that fateful September 11 brought the destruction of the World Trade Center. All the signs were there for the noting—the 1993 bombing of the World Trade Center; attacks against American embassies in Africa; the bombing of the USS *Cole* in Yemen; bombing of the U.S. military barracks in Saudi Arabia... My first *Delta* manuscript, *Detachment Delta: Punitive Strike*, reached editor Jennifer Fisher at Avon five days before 9-11, eliciting her comment that,

"There was an eerie sense of wondering what was fact and what was fiction..."

With wife Donna Sue salmon fishing in Alaska.

The second *Delta* novel, *Detachment Delta: Operation Iron Weed,* unveils a secret behind Osama bin Laden which apparently turned out to be a true prediction. The third, *Detachment Delta: Operation Deep Steel*, was written before the 2003 War on Iraq, Operation *Iraqi Freedom*, and the nuclear confrontation with North Korea. It involves a scenario eerily presaging the crisis.

All this was made possible because of *Research* and *Marketing.*

One important but neglected aspect of freelancer marketing has to do with the writer's relationship with agents, editors and publishers. A good working alliance with them is vital if you hope to continue in this business and be successful. Hard-to-work-with writers soon find themselves twiddling their thumbs and tacking rejection slips to the wall.

A very famous personality whose co-authored novels have been New York *Times* bestsellers for several years is about to crash. He is so difficult to work with that he would have been gone long ago except for the professional writers who actually produce his books. Even they are deserting him, unable to deal with his abrasive and demanding personality. I turned down offers three times to co-author his novels. His last two books—ghost-written—failed dismally. He'll soon fade from view.

One last facet of marketing concerns diversity—diversity of talent and output, not political correctness diversity. I want to get as much mileage as possible out of my research, which means marketing it to a variety of outlets. Although it is perfectly ethical to re-work an article for sale to non-competing markets, I rarely do it, primarily because I don't have time. However, I do use the same materials for more than one article or book.

My research on forest fires led to *Smoke Jumpers* and to an article in *Adventure West* magazine. *The 100<sup>th</sup> Kill,* a novel, evolved out of *One Shot-One Kill*, nonfiction. That research also produced articles in *Vietnam, Modern Warfare* and *Guns & Ammo* magazines. My research on political correctness generated a novel, *Liberty City,* a nonfiction book, *Going Bonkers: The Wacky World of Cultural Madness,* and, so far, articles for *Soldier of Fortune* and *The Scavenger Newsletter.*

"If you are a writer (with marketing skills)," *Writer's Market 2003* suggested, "then you have a good chance at becoming a paid, published writer who will reap the benefits of a long and successful career."

### 

"Publicity and promotion are the great equalizers for the little publisher or the unheralded writer," asserted Tom and Marilyn Ross in their *The Complete Guide to Self-Publishing.*

Promotion, translated as salesmanship, can literally mean the difference between a book's success and its failure. Promotion is usually more important than the book itself, a fact about the business that can shake up the writer more than any other. I understand this fully. Nonetheless, in spite of everything, I am rather a shy man and loathe to promote myself overtly. I prefer to stand by the old adage that if I build a better mouse trap the world will beat a path to my door.

Having said that, I still do not recommend such a philosophy for the new writer. Since most publishers can afford to promote only a few of their stars, you can promote yourself and out-compete even the largest publishing houses. If you have a telephone, a computer, and a car, you can generate loads of free publicity that will pay off in sales. You don't have to hire expensive public relations agencies; most writers can't afford them anyhow. Below are a few simple steps you can take to promote your own book.

Start out be sending photocopies of your pre-published book to well-known authorities and experts familiar with your book's genre or subject matter, endorsements and favorable comments from whom can be displayed on the cover to attract the attention of book store browsers. Jim Morris, for example, endorsed the front cover of *The 100$^{th}$ Kill* with "Few men know men or war as well as Chuck Sasser." For the cover of *Taking Fire*, W.E.B. Griffin wrote, "Containing some of the best writing in the field...an electrifying glimpse into the dangerous life of a chopper pilot in Vietnam." In return, I have endorsed books for authors like Mark D. Harrell, Beatrice D. Harrell (no kin to Mark), M.E. Cooper, Patti Dickinson, and others.

Quotes sell books.

Celebrity Forwards for your book also generate interest. Colonel David H. Hackworth (*About Face; Steel My Soldiers' Hearts*) wrote a Forward for my *Doc: Platoon Medic*. I wrote, among others, the Forward for *Barbara: The Story of A UFO Investigator* by Barbara Bartholic and Peggy Fielding.

Never spend money for advertising when you can get it free. Once the cover art is ready for your book, usually about five months before publication, reproduce the front and back covers on a one-sheet promotional flyer. Add a press release about the book, along with an Author's Biography, and mail out to newspapers, magazines, TV talk shows, and radio stations that you think might be interested. National is good, but since most national media outlets are deluged with promotional materials it might be best to concentrate on local and regional targets instead. They are generally more eager to cooperate.

Once the book is published, you might send out review copies to selected magazines, newspapers and broadcast outlets. It'll cost you a few bucks, but this is generally one of the most cost-effective ways to generate publicity and sales. At the same time, make yourself available to speak before writers groups, civic organization, clubs and other gatherings. Make sure you have a book signing afterwards.

You may even want to go on a book signing tour preceded by media events, kicked off perhaps by a Book Party in your hometown. Your best bet, economical-wise, is to contact book stores within a 150-mile radius of home. That way you can drive to and from the event without worrying about the expenses of overnight lodging and eating out. Make sure all media within the radius receive press release packets at least two weeks in advance and that you arrange for interviews and appearances. The best scenario for results is to have media coverage about 48 hours in advance of a signing.

In 2001 when I made the first transcontinental flight by powered parachute, I arranged in advance to sign books each afternoon and evening when I landed. TV, radio, and print media frequently met me at the airport or at the landing field when I touched down. The adventure generated excitement, which in turn mustered activity for book signings. I signed books in 23 different cities from San Diego to Jacksonville, Florida.

Finally, don't forget online. More than 90 percent of Americans have online access and a healthy percentage of them want to know about your book. You can use a cyber friend or a "Dummies" book to help you build a website and link it to other sites.

Successful writers know that publishing requires two different mind sets. The first is the actual writing, the second is the business of writing—Research, Marketing and Promotion. Both mind sets must be handled with equal facility if you ever expect to move out of that tool shed in the woods.

# CONCLUSION

A book packager is someone who puts together ideas for books and series, sells them to a publisher, then recruits writers to produce the books. Bill Fawcett is a book packager, in addition to being a successful author himself. In 2000, he contacted me about writing a novel, the second in a series about Navy SEALs. There was only one catch.

"I have to have the manuscript in *four* weeks."

He explained how, for some reason, the writer he originally recruited to author the second book in the series hadn't produced. It was now final quarter, two minutes to the bell, and the ball was in the other court. It was formula writing, but nonetheless a daunting task to writer 100,000 words in four weeks while giving myself time for my usual one rewrite.

By this point in my career, I had developed my skills so I could concentrate on writing the story without having to go through the conscious process of applying the tools. I was comfortable with the hammers and saws of the writer's craft and I had mastered, at least to some degree, the five magic steps on the pathway to writing success.

"I decided a long time ago that writers should not be encouraged," Erskine Caldwell wrote. "They should be discouraged. That's more helpful to a writer than encouragement, because I think he's going to learn a lot more that way. If you are going to be a writer, you will be, encouraged or not."

He's right. If you are going to be a writer, you will be, no matter what. If a poor kid from an illiterate family out of the hills can make it as a writer, you can too—providing you apply these five broad principles I have outlined in this book.

*Discipline:* "Work every day," Ernest Hemingway counseled. "No matter what happened the day or night before, get up and bite the nail."

*Inspiration:* We must believe that at least some of the inner voices playing around inside our writer heads might interest other people. We mustn't be trembling and apologetic about our work. We must depend upon a tough inner core to drive us and not listen to those who would steal our dreams.

*Goals:* There are very few Stephen Kings, John Grishams or Anne Rices. That level of commercial success in writing is rare—but it is not impossible. You have to believe that. You have to at least reach for the moon. You never get anything you don't reach for. You reach every destination by merely taking one step at a time.

*Ideas:* "And so," Gore Vidal wrote, "from one sentence came the next sentence. Then you weave the sentences together, and the sentences have their own kinetic energy. It's like Baron Frankenstein's electrical machine; suddenly the clay monster of language gets filled with life and sits up..."

*Craft:* "There are techniques and skills to be learned for writing as in any other profession or trade," said Louis L'Amour. These skills and techniques, learned, flesh out the other four principles and provide the would-be writer the means to eliminate "would-be" and *become* a writer.

In this book I have discussed the qualities I believe necessary for the new or aspiring writer to find success in communicating through the printed word. I hope to have been able to bring some illumination into that lonely circle of light in which writers spend so much of our lives. I hope this book has helped you to map out your dreams. It is from such dreams seeping from lonely circles of light that we ensure that darkness shall never envelope the world.

# Charles W. Sasser

Stay up-to-date on the latest from Charles W. Sasser by going to his web site, http://www.CharlesSasser.com and joining his mailing list. (It's free.)

**More writing books from AWOC.COM**

*The Complete Guide to Writing & Selling Magazine Articles by Peggy Fielding and Dan Case – US $19.95 –* The definitive guide for those who write for magazines. Over 300 markets are included.

*Be Your Own Book Doctor by Robin Conley – US $9.95 –* Learn to be your own book doctor so you can cure what ails your writing.

*Confessing for Money by Peggy Fielding – US $14.95 –* Writing and selling to the **SECRET** short story market.

To purchase these titles, go online to AWOCBooks.com or send a check or money order for the purchase price plus US $4.00 for S & H (Canada US $5.50) to:

AWOC Books
P.O. Box 2819
Denton, TX 76202